The Coaches Collection
of
SOCCER
DRILLS

To Janice and Diane
who have waited patiently
through many practice sessions

The Coaches Collection of
SOCCER DRILLS

by
John A. Reeves
Drew University
and
J. Malcolm Simon
New Jersey Institute of Technology

LEISURE PRESS

Champaign, Illinois

Leisure Press
A Division of Human Kinetics
P.O. Box 5076, Champaign, IL 61825-5076
1-800-747-4457

Canada:
Human Kinetics
Box 24040, Windsor, ON N8Y 4Y9
1-800-465-7301 (in Canada only)

Europe:
Human Kinetics
P.O. Box IW14, Leeds LS16 6TR, United Kingdom
(44) 1132 781708

Australia:
Human Kinetics
2 Ingrid Street, Clapham 5062, South Australia
(08) 371 3755

New Zealand:
Human Kinetics
P.O. Box 105-231, Auckland 1
(09) 523 3462

Library of Congress Catalog Card No. 80-84212
ISBN-0-918438-63-2
10   9

Front cover photograph: David Madison, Inc.
Back cover design: Rocco Campanella

Test photographs: courtesy of the Stanford University Sports Publicity Department

CONTENTS

PREFACE

The growth of soccer in the United States, particularly in recent years, has been phenomenal. This growth is reflected by the ever increasing number of soccer teams representing recreational programs, elementary schools, junior high schools, secondary schools, colleges and universities, and amateur and professional leagues. The corresponding increase of coaches has created a need for aids to facilitate instruction and coaching. The purpose of this publication is to aid coaches in the selection and planning of soccer drills which are essential to effective practice sessions.

The importance of drills cannot be overemphasized. A coach cannot expect a player to perform a skill if that skill has not been learned through adequate practice. A skill, once learned, can then be performed almost automatically. However, to achieve this automatic level of performance, much practice is necessary with planned progression from simple movements to complex situations. Well planned drills are the best means of such development and will provide the player with a sound base for future learning.

It is not enough to employ one, two or even a few favorite drills over and over. Players will learn better if not bored by a lack of variety in the practice program. This collection provides a large selection of drills to which each coach can add his own favorites. Most of the drills have been created or collected by the authors during their combined forty-two years as college soccer coaches. Other drills included have been submitted by some of the most successful college coaches in the United States.

The drills are indexed in four different ways; (1) alphabetically by title, (2) according to the primary emphasis, (3) according to either primary or secondary emphasis, and (4) by the name of the contributing coach if other than the authors.

The authors are grateful to those coaches who contributed to this collection of drills. We also express our appreciation to Mary Monaco for the preparation of this manuscript; and to Rocco Campanella, a soccer player and recent graduate of the School of Architecture at New Jersey Institute of Technology, for designing the back cover.

John A. Reeves and J. Malcolm Simon

INDEX OF DRILLS

DRILL   **DRILL NUMBER**

INDEX OF PRIMARY EMPHASES

INDEX OF PRIMARY AND SECONDARY EMPHASES

INDEX OF CONTRIBUTING AUTHORS

CONTRIBUTOR	INSTITUTION	DRILL NUMBER
Athey, Ed	Washington College	36
Bacon, Fran	University of Bridgeport	26
Bahr, Walter	The Pennsylvania State University	73
Boles, John	Temple University	61
Cervasio, Ron	Boston University	106
Coven, Michael	Brandeis University	17
Eck, Joseph	Sangamon State University	15
Fager, Russ	Rider College	96
Goldman, Howard	Marist College	70
Griffith, Thomas	Dartmouth College	135
Griggs, Steve	Yale University	80
Guelker, Bob	Southern Illinois University—Edwardsville	38
Gross, Larry M.	North Carolina State University	83
Henni, Geza	University of Rhode Island	78
Hindley, Gary	Trenton State College	71
Howell, Gordie	Rollins College	16
Ibrahim, I.M.	Clemson University	25
Kline, Loren	University of Delaware	134
Lewis, Bud	Wilmington College	39
Logan, George R.	San Diego State University	108
Martin, Jay	Ohio Wesleyan University	84
McCrath, C. Cliff	Seattle Pacific University	93
Miller, Jay	Tampa University	4
Morrone, Joe	University of Connecticut	76
Muse, William	Princeton University	121
Myers, Will	William Paterson College	72
Rennie, John	Duke University	67
Rogers, William	Babson College	46
Sagastume, Luis A.	U.S. Air Force Academy	75
Schmalz, Fred	University of Evansville	110
Schum, Tim	State University of N.Y. at Binghamton	48
Seddon, Robert	University of Pennsylvania	32
Shewgraft, Ron	North Adams State College	45
Werner, Helmut	Randolph Macon College	85
Wright, Owen	Elizabethtown College	95

DRILLS
#1-136

1 BACK TO BASICS

Shooting   20 yd. by 20 yd.   4-24 Players   12 Balls
                 Area in Front of Goal

Passing

Formation: Field players form two lines at the outer corners of the penalty
area. One line of players is supplied with balls. A field player
stands in the center of the goal.

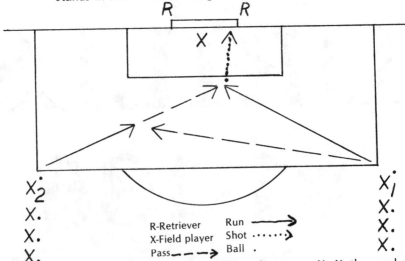

R-Retriever   Run ——→
X-Field player Shot ·····→
Pass— — —→   Ball ·

Procedure: X_1 passes diagonally across the penalty area to X_2. X_1 then makes
a run towards the goal, receives a return pass from X_2, and
shoots on goal. The passes should be controlled ground passes
designed to be converted into a sure goal. The field player
guarding the goal must stay on the goal line in the center of the
goal and may only use his feet to stop a score. To limit the
possibility of miskicks, shooters are encouraged to use the inside
of the foot. The player guarding the goal is changed frequently.
X_1 and X_2 go to the end of the opposite line after their turn.

Variation: 1. Demand ten consecutive scores.
2. Players providing a poor pass or missing a shot after a good
   pass run a lap around the field.
3. All play must be one touch.
4. Start with balls in left line so that the shots come from the
   left side.

2 BALL CONTROL

Dribbling   Center Circle   6-12 Players   6-12 Balls

Shielding

Formation: Each player, in possession of a ball, is in the center circle.

O-Offensive player
Ball .

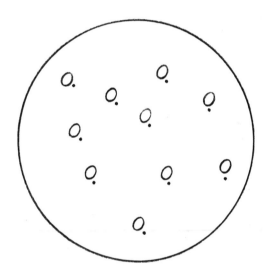

Procedure: At a signal all players dribble within the center circle. While dribbling, each player attempts to kick the ball of other players out of the center circle while preventing other players from doing the same to his ball. The drill continues until only one player remains in the circle in possession of his ball.

3 BE AGGRESSIVE

Tackling Penalty Area 6-12 Players 1 Balls

2 Small
Goals

Offensive and
Defensive Techniques

Formation: Six players occupy a small area such as the penalty area. If small
goals are not available, cones can be used.

X-Field player

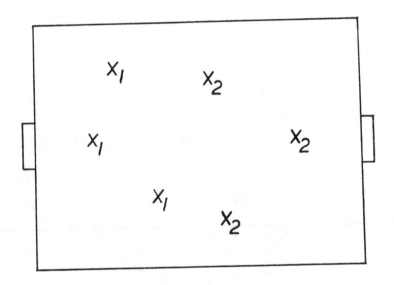

Procedure: Start with a three vs three game and increase size of teams as
desired.

Variation: To force a great deal of tackling practice under competitive
conditions, the game can be played under one of the following
restrictions:
1. The player in possession must try to beat an opponent by
dribbling before he can make a pass.
2. The player in possession dribbles the ball until he loses it or
gets a shot on goal.

4 BEAT THAT PASS

Fitness   ½ Field or less   8 Players   1 Ball

1 Cone

Passing
Throwing

CONTRIBUTOR: Jay Miller, Tampa University, Tampa, Florida 33606

Formation: Players X_1 through X_6 form a line. A cone is placed at a distance of ten to twenty yards in front of the line (the distance will depend upon how much sprinting is desired and the distance that the ball is being kicked). X_8 is about forty yards from start and X_7 is stationed near the cone.

X-Field player
Pass -- -->
Run ----->
Cone ⊙

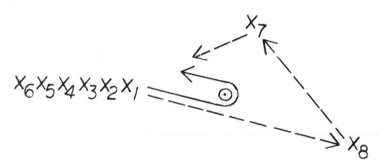

Procedure: X_1 kicks the ball forward past X_8, if possible. X_1 then sprints around the cone and back to the start. Meanwhile X_8, who may be a field player or goalkeeper, retrieves the ball and attempts to hit X_1 or throw it to X_7 to hit X_1 before he returns to the start. If desired, score may be kept. Score one point for the sprinter if he gets back to start without being hit, or one point for the retrievers if the sprinter is hit before returning to start.

5 BEAT THE KEEPER

Goalkeeping   10 yd. by 20 yd. Area   2 Players   1 Ball

Goalkeeper

Heading

Formation: A goalkeeper is in the middle of the area with two players, one with a ball, at opposite ends of the area.

G-Goalkeeper
X-Field player
Pass— — —➔
Shot· · · · · · · ·➔
Ball .

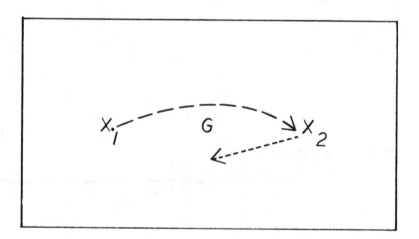

Procedure: X₁ throws or chips the ball to X₂ who heads the ball in an attempt to pass the goalkeeper. The goalkeeper should be facing X₁ and then turn to save the head shot by X₂. Later, the goalkeeper should be facing X₂ all the time.

24

6 BEAT THEM ALL

Offensive and Defensive Techniques	100 yd. by 15 yd. Area	8-12 Players	3 Balls 8 Cones

---

Formation: A rectangular area one hundred yards by fifteen yards is marked with cones. Cones are placed at twenty yard intervals within the one hundred yard area. Offensive players line up at the entrance to the course. Defensive players position themselves between the width of the course at twenty yard intervals.

D-Defensive player
O-Offensive Player
Dribble ∿∿∿➤
Run ───➤
Cone ◐

⊙   ⊙

D   *D*   *D*   *D*   *D*➝ ⟵∿*O OOO*

⊙   ⊙   ⊙   ⊙   ⊙   ⊙

Procedure: An offensive player dribbles toward the first defensive player who advances from the first cone (twenty yards from start) and attempts to tackle the ball. The offensive player attempts to beat the defensive player and, if successful, continues to advance to confront the next defensive player. The offensive player continues until he beats five defenders in order or until he loses possession of the ball. After the offensive player completes his turn he becomes a defensive player at cone five while all other defensemen move up one cone. The defensive player who started at cone one goes to the end of the waiting line of offensive players.

7 BOMBARDMENT

Heading   Penalty Area   12 Players   6 Balls

                                                               1 Goal

---

Formation: There are two teams of six players each. Three defenders guard
the goal and goal area from six attackers who are stationed outside the penalty area. The other three defenders stay behind the
goal and return balls to the attackers. The defenders are rotated
after a specified number of shots.

D-Defensive player
O-Offensive player
R-Retriever

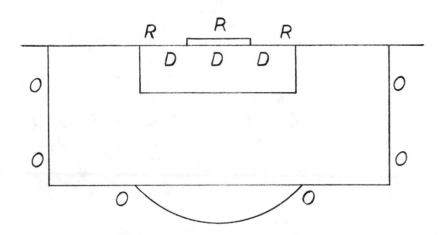

Procedure: The attackers, one at a time, or any number at one time, lob or
chip balls to the goal area. The defenders try to prevent the balls
from going in the goal or landing in the goal area.

One point is scored for each ball touching ground in the goal
area; two points for scoring a goal.

After a specified number of attempts, the teams switch
assignments.

8 CAPITALIZE ON A MISTAKE

Shooting   Penalty Area   12 Players   10 Balls

Goalkeeper

Goalkeeping

Formation: Players form two lines approximately ten yards from and facing a goal. A goalkeeper is in goal. A feeder, who may be a player, stands between the two lines.

F-Feeder
G-Goalkeeper
O-Offensive player
Run ———⟶
Shot. . . . . . ⟩

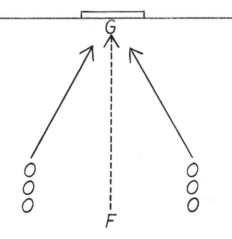

Procedure: The feeder shoots balls to a spot within the reach of the goalkeeper. Shots are taken hard so that the goalkeeper will have difficulty handling them. A second or two before each shot is taken the first player in each line sprints at the goalkeeper. The objective of the offensive players is to convert dropped balls into goals. Shots are taken rapidly so that players keep moving. The goalkeeper rolls cleanly played balls back to the feeder. Offensive players go to the end of the opposite line after each turn, and the feeder is switched periodically.

9 CAT AND MOUSE

Marking Penalty Area 12 Players 12 Balls

Goalkeeper 1 Goal

Containment

Formation: Four lines of attackers and defenders are on opposite sides of the penalty area starting at the corners furthest from the goal. Each attacker should have a ball. The goalkeeper is in goal.

D-Defensive player
G-Goalkeeper
O-Offensive player
Dribble ⌇⌇⌇➤
Run————➤
Shot········➤
Ball.

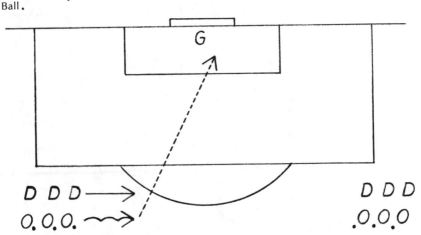

Procedure: Starting from one corner, O dribbles across the penalty area trying to get free for a shot on goal. D tries to stay goal side of O to prevent a good shot. Play continues until a shot is taken or O loses possession of the ball.

The players move to the ends of their respective lines at the opposite corner and the first O and D from that line continue the drill.

After a specified time or number of attempts, the players should switch assignments.

10 CIRCLE KEEP AWAY

Passing	Center Circle or Similar Area	5-12 Players	1 Ball

Defensive
Techniques

Formation: Players form a large circle with one player within the circle.

D-Defensive player
O-Offensive player
Pass _ _ _ _ ➔

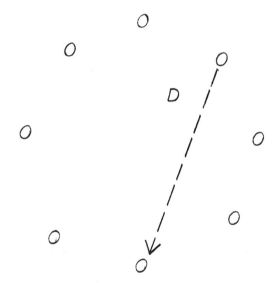

Procedure: The ball is passed among the players forming the circle. The player in the center attempts to intercept a pass. If the player within the circle succeeds in touching the ball, the player who last played the ball assumes the role of the player within the circle while the player formerly in the center joins the players on the circle.

Variation: 1. Players forming the circle may pass first time.
2. Two players play defense within the circle.

11 CIRCLE SPRINT

Fitness   Center Circle   1-12 Players   9 Cones

Formation: Players stand outside two cones which are designated as the starting point. Seven more cones are placed at equal distances around center circle.

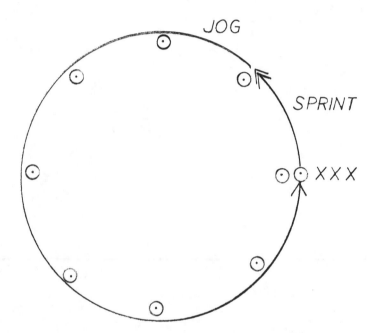

Procedure: At a signal, players sprint from start to first cone, then jog around circle to start. Players now sprint from start to second cone and then jog to the start. This continues until the players sprint around the entire circle.

12 CIRCLE TO SHOOT

Shooting	25 yds. in front of a Goal	12-24 Players	12 Balls
			Goal

Formation: One half of the group lines up behind one of the goal posts. The other half of the group spreads out and serves as retrievers. A feeder, at the eighteen, spots or lobs the ball for the oncoming players. A cone is placed about five yards past the feeder. A goalkeeper is in the goal.

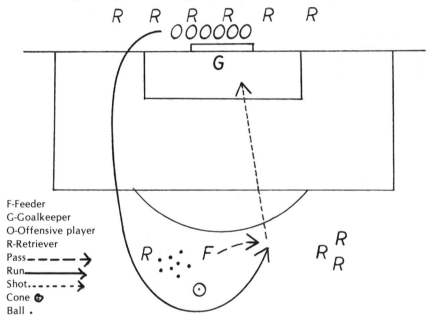

F-Feeder
G-Goalkeeper
O-Offensive player
R-Retriever
Pass ----→
Run ----→
Shot ------→
Cone ☻
Ball .

Procedure: The one half of the group that is shooting continuously runs in a large circle from the post, around the cone, and back behind the goal. After passing the cone each shooter receives a ball from the feeder and shoots on goal. After a prescribed period of time (two minutes is suggested), the shooters become retrievers and the retrievers shoot.

Variation: 1. Offensive players line up at the other post and shoot with other foot.
2. The feeder lofts the ball higher and the shot is taken on the volley or headed on goal.

13 CLEARING HIGH BALLS

Clearing   ½ Field   2-12 Players   10 Balls

                              Goalkeeper

Communication
Punting

Formation: Field players form two lines ten yards apart. A goalkeeper faces
the lines 50 yards away. A cone is placed five yards to the side
and in front of each line of players.

G-Goalkeeper
X-Field player
Pass — — — →
Run ——————→
Ball •
Cone ◎

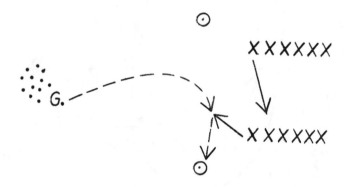

Procedure: A goalkeeper lofts a punt, drop kick or throw to the area between the two lines of players. One of the first players in each
line calls for the ball and clears, attempting to hit one of the two
targets (cones). The other field player involved backs up the
player clearing the ball. The player backing up retrieves the ball
and returns it to the goalkeeper. Field players go to the end of
the opposite line after their turn is complete.

14 CLOSE MARKING

Marking

Control
Shielding

Any Open Area   2-24 Players   1 Ball per
pair

Formation: Pairs of players spread out. One player in each pair has a ball at
his feet.

X-Field player
Ball .

$X_1.$ X_2

$X_5.$ X_6

$X_3.$ X_4

Procedure: At a signal the player of each pair with the ball dribbles, protect-
ing the ball with his body. The other player in the pair attempts
to mark closely. If, after a period of thirty to sixty seconds, the
player without the ball is close enough to touch the player with
the ball, he has succeeded in marking closely.

Variation: 1. The marking player attempts to take the ball from the other
player in the pair.

15 COMMUNICATING

Communication   20 yd. Area   3 Players   1 Ball

Control

CONTRIBUTOR: Joseph Eck, Sangamon State University, Springfield,
Illinois 62708

Formation: Three players form a straight line with X₃, in the middle, ten
yards from X₁ and X₂.

X-Field player
Pass — — — — →
Ball ▪

Procedure: The object of the drill is for the passer to tell the player receiving
the ball what to do. X_1 passes to X_3 and calls, "carry, turn, man
on, or one-time." X_3 reacts according to the specific command.
For example, if X_1 calls, "man-on", X_3 immediately passes the
ball back to X_1. If X_1 calls, "carry", X_3 turns, carries and passes
the ball to X_2. X_2 then passes the ball back to X_3 and tells him
what to do. Play continues, with the ball constantly moving, for
one minute. The players then change positions.

Variation: 1. The outside players use throw-ins to the middle player.

34

16 CONFINED ATTACK

Offensive	Penalty Area	8 Players	6 Balls
Techniques			
		Goalkeeper	Goal

Defensive Techniques
Goalkeeping

CONTRIBUTOR: Gordie Howell, Rollins College, Winter Park, Florida 32789

Formation: Four offensive players and four defensive players are in the penalty area. A goalkeeper is in the goal. A feeder with 6 balls stands outside the penalty area.

D-Defensive player
F-Feeder
G-Goalkeeper
O-Offensive player
Pass — — — — →
Ball .

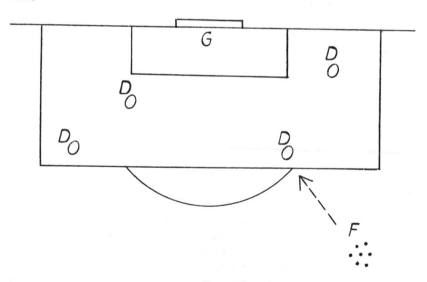

Procedure: Four offensive players attack against four defensive players for four minutes. The feeder serves another ball to an offensive player each time a ball goes out of play. Defenders must play man to man.

17 CONTINUOUS SHOOTING

Shooting   Penalty Area   4 or more   1 Ball
                            Players   per player

                                         Goal

CONTRIBUTOR: Michael Coven, Brandeis University, Waltham, Massachusetts 02254

Formation: Players, each with a ball, form lines to the side and behind each goalpost.

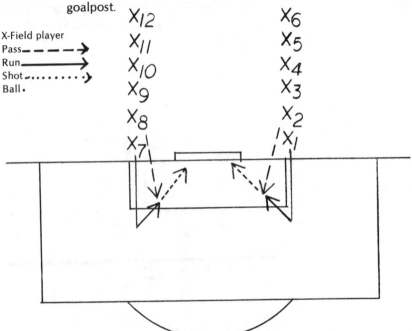

X-Field player
Pass$- - - \rightarrow$
Run$\longrightarrow$
Shot$\cdots\cdots\cdots\rightarrow$
Ball $\bullet$

Procedure: X_1 and X_7 make straight runs from the end line to about the six yard line where they turn to the goal. X_2 passes to the left foot of X_1, while X_8 passes to the right foot of X_7. X_1 and X_7 shoot first time to the upper corner of the goal nearest each of them. After shooting, X_1 and X_7 move to the end of the opposite line and everyone moves up one spot.

Variation: The ball may be thrown to the player turning at the six yard line so that he may head the ball into the near corner.

36

18 CONTINUOUS SHORT PASS

Passing   10 yd. by 10 yd. Area   4-16 Players   1-3 Balls

Fitness

Formation: Field players form two lines 5 yards apart from, and to the side of, each other.

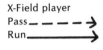

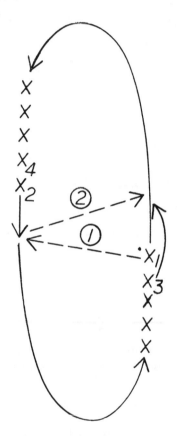

Procedure: Player X₁ passes diagonally to player X₂ who passes one touch to player X₃, etc. Play continues. Players go to the end of the opposite line after passing.

Variation: Place two cones between the lines and demand that the passes go through this confined area.

19 CONTROL PRESSURE

Control   50 yd. by 50 yd. Area   5 Players   2 Balls

Passing

Formation: Four players are located about thirty to forty yards from each other. Two players, X_2 and X_3, each have a ball.

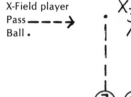

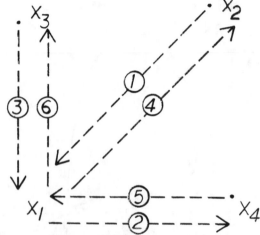

Procedure: One player at a time is put under pressure. The drill starts when X_2 makes a lofted pass (1) to X_1 who must control with one touch and, on the second touch, pass the ball (2) to X_4, the free player. As soon as the first ball is controlled by X_1, X_3 makes the next pass (3). X_1 must again control and pass to the free player, now X_2. The drill continues in the same manner (passes 5 & 6) with a new free player each time.

The player under pressure is changed after a set time period or number of passes, and a specific rotation order should be used.

The passes to X_1 should be in the air and should force him to move to the ball and use different control techniques.

Variation: Better players should be challenged by increasing the pressure on them.
1. Passes can be made faster and more difficult to control.
2. The free players can make runs off the ball while the pass is being made to the player under pressure.
3. A fifth player can provide opposition on the player under pressure. This pressure can be passive at first and increased to game-like conditions.

20 COVER THREE GOALS

Goalkeeping   10 yd. by 10 yd. Area   1 Goalkeeper   9 Balls

3 Cones

Formation: A triangle of cones is set up. Cones are placed five yards apart. A goalkeeper stands between two of the cones. A feeder with a supply of balls stands between and five to ten yards away from each pair of cones.

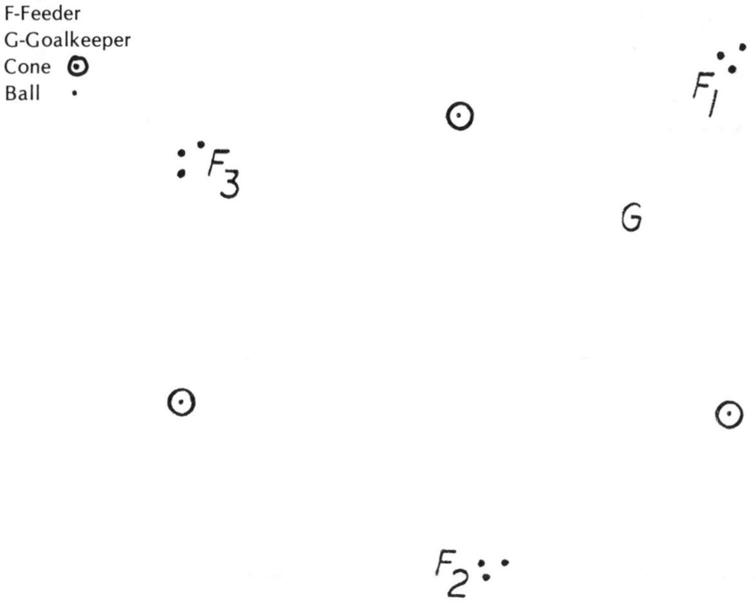

F-Feeder
G-Goalkeeper
Cone ⊙
Ball ·

⊙

F_1

F_3

G

⊙

⊙

F_2

Procedure: Feeder F_1 shoots on goal. The goalkeeper attempts to make the save. After the attempt the goalkeeper moves counter-clockwise to the next goal. F_2 attempts to score. The drill proceeds for a prescribed time.

21 DEFENSIVE CONTAINMENT

Defensive	10 yd. by 5 yd. Area	12 Players	1 Ball
Techniques			
			4 Cones
			Stopwatch

Formation: A rectangle ten yards by five yards is formed using four cones. Six offensive players are in line ready to dribble the ball through the rectangle while six defensive players are in line ready to confront, in turn, the player with the ball.

D-Defensive player
O-Offensive player
Dribble 〰〰〰➤
Run————➤
Ball ·
Cone ◉

◉   ◉

$$D\ D\ D\ D \longrightarrow \qquad \longleftarrow\!\!\sim\!\!\sim\!\!O\ O\ O\ O$$

◉   ◉

Procedure: The offensive player attempts to dribble the ball a distance of ten yards through the area marked by the cones. The defensive player attempts to delay the offensive players within the cones for ten seconds.

22 DEFENSIVE PRESSURE

Clearing   Penalty Area   7 or More Players   8 Balls

1 Goal

Formation: Four feeders, each with two soccer balls, are located at the four corners of the penalty area. One defender is located in the goal area, and two attackers are located in different positions within the penalty area. Other players serve as retrievers behind the goal.

D-Defensive player
F-Feeder
G-Goalkeeper
O-Offensive player
R-Retriever
Pass — — — —→
Ball .

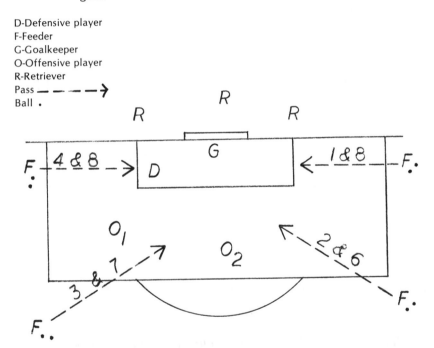

Procedure: The defender is put under pressure as the two attackers alternate in fighting for balls being passed by the feeders. Starting at one corner, the first pass (F_1) is made. O_1 and D fight for the ball. As soon as the ball is cleared, shot, goes out of bounds or the goalkeeper gain possession, the second pass (F_2) is made with O_2 and D fighting for it. This order continues until eight passes are made, after which all players rotate to a new position. The passes should be made so that both the attacker and defender have a reasonable chance to play the ball.

23 DEFENSIVE RECOVERY

Offensive and ½ Field 4-12 Players 6 Balls
Defensive Techniques

Goalkeeper

Formation: Players form defensive and offensive lines at midfield. A feeder is between the lines. A goalkeeper is in goal.

D-Defensive player
F-Feeder
G-Goalkeeper
O-Offensive player
Pass_ _ _ _ _→
Run_____→
Ball.

Procedure: The first defensive player in line faces the feeder two yards in front of him. The feeder kicks the ball between the legs of the defensive player. As the kick is taken the offensive player sprints to gain control and shoot on goal. After the ball travels through the legs of the defensive player he turns and attempts to recover to play defense against the offensive player. The players retrieve the ball and go to the end of the opposite line after each turn.

Variation: Eliminate the feeder and have the first offensive player pass through the legs of the defender.

24 DEFLECTED SHOT

Goalkeeping   Penalty Area   1 Goalkeeper   10 Balls

                                                                    12 Cones

---

Formation: A goalkeeper is in the goal. Twelve cones are strewn in front of the goalkeeper. A feeder with several balls is at the penalty mark.

F-Feeder
G-Goalkeeper
Shot . . . . . .>
Ball   .
Cone ☉

G

☉ ☉ ☉ ☉ ☉ ☉

☉ ☉ ☉ ☉ ☉ ☉

F· · · · •

Procedure: The feeder shoots on goal through the cones. The goalkeeper attempts to save balls deflected by hitting the cones.

25 DENY THROUGH PASS

Passing   10 yd by 10 yd Area   6 Players   1 Ball

Defensive Techniques

CONTRIBUTOR: I.M. Ibrahim, Clemson University, Clemson, South Carolina
        29631

Formation: Four offensive players position themselves in a square about ten to fifteen yards apart. Two defensive players are within the square formed by the offensive players.

D-Defensive player
O-Offensive player
Pass _ _ _ _ →
Ball •

Procedure: Offensive players pass the ball among themselves and score a point if a through pass (to the player diagonally across) is completed. Defensive players score a point each time they intercept a pass.

Variation: (Two touch) Offensive players may control and pass.
(One touch) Offensive players must pass without controlling the ball.

26 DEVELOPMENT OF TOUCH

Dribbling   50 yd. by 40 yd. Area   16 or More   6 Balls
                                              Players

Control

CONTRIBUTOR: Fran Bacon, University of Bridgeport, Bridgeport,
                 Connecticut 06602

Formation: Four balls are placed in a line ten yards apart from each other
and twenty yards across from four other balls. Players form lines
behind the ball with at least two players in each line. From this
formation players move in various directions with the ball.

X-Field player
Dribble 〰〰〰➤
Ball •

Procedure: The first player in each line dribbles toward the player directly
opposite him. When the players meet in the middle they ex-
change balls and proceed to the other side. The second player
and subsequent players in turn continue the drill.

Variation: 1. The first player in each line dribbles toward and exchanges balls with the player diagonally across from him.

2. Use only four balls. Narrow distance between players to ten yards. One player dribbles to the center. Exchange is made and the other player dribbles across to other side.

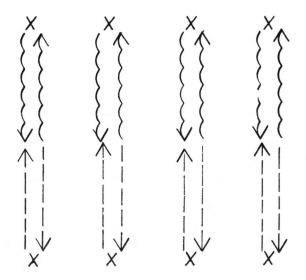

27 DOG DRILL

Offensive and ½ Field 12 Players 6 Balls
Defensive
Techniques Goalkeeper

Fitness

Formation: There are two lines of players on opposite sides of the center circle. Each attacker should have a ball. A goalkeeper is in goal.

D-Defensive player
G-Goalkeeper
O-Offensive player
Dribble ∿∿∿➤
Run ———➤
Shot ------➤
Ball .

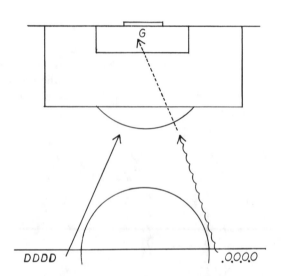

Procedure: On the coach's signal, O moves as fast as possible on goal with the ball. As soon as O takes two steps, D chases him. O tries to get off a shot on goal before D catches him, but no closer than the penalty area.

If D catches O, D tries to prevent a good shot or tries to take the ball away. If successful in gaining possession, D must pass the ball to the goalkeeper or take it out to the side. Play continues until the shot is taken or the defense has clear possession. Players then retrieve the ball and move to the end of the opposite line.

28 DRIBBLE AND EVADE

Dribbling   10 yd. by 10 yd. Area   4 Players   4 Balls

Formation: Four players, each with a ball, are inside the 10 yd. × 10 yd. area.

X-Field player
Ball •

X.

X.   .X

X.

Procedure: To develop the idea of dribbling in confined areas and creating space in congestion, the players, while continually dribbling, are to run at another player, fake, evade the player and dribble to a line of the area.

29 DRIBBLE SHUTTLE

Dribbling   25 yd. Area   4 or More Players   5 Balls

Fitness

Formation: Five balls are lined up at five yard intervals, the first ball five yards from a start line. The players line up behind the start line.

X-Field player
Dribble 〰〰〰➤
Run ————➤
Ball •

Procedure: On signal, X sprints to the first ball, dribbles it back to start and leaves it there. He repeats this procedure until all the balls, in order, are collected and dribbled to start. If all the balls are brought to start before the time limit, he now returns the balls to their marks, also one at a time. After forty-five seconds, record the number of balls brought back to start and returned to their marks.

Variation: This can be performed as a relay race with the first player bringing the ball back to start, the second player returning them to their marks, and so on.

30 DRIBBLE SPRINT

Fitness   35 yd. by 20 yd.   2-12 Players   2 Balls

Dribbling

Formation: Two lines of players face a course thirty yards long. Cones are placed at five yard intervals in front of a starting line. Two players run the course at a time.

X-Player
Dribble
Cone

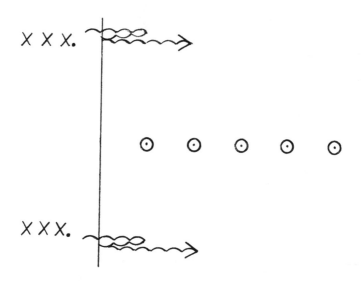

Procedure: The first player in each line dribbles as fast as possible to the first cone and back to the start. He then dribbles to the second cone and back to the start, etc., until the entire course is completed, after which the next two players go, and so on until players complete the course.

Variation: 1. The course may be run without a ball.
2. The run may be timed creating competition between players and motivation to achieve personal best times.

31 DROP PASS FOR SHOT

Shooting   ½ Field   6-18 Field Players   6 Balls

Goalkeeper

Passing

Formation: Two lines of offensive players form at mid-field. One line is supplied with balls. A line of defensive players forms behind one of the goals posts. A goalkeeper is in goal.

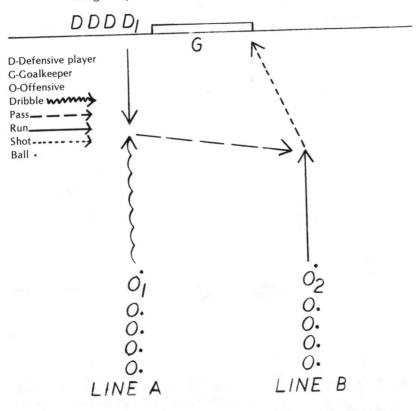

D D D D|

G

D-Defensive player
G-Goalkeeper
O-Offensive
Dribble
Pass
Run
Shot
Ball ·

O₁

O.

O.

O.

O.

LINE A

O₂

O.

O.

O.

O.

LINE B

Procedure: The first player from line A, O₁, dribbles to about the eighteen yard line. When confronted by a defensive player, he drops a diagonal pass for O₂ who has timed his run to meet the pass and take a powerful first time shot. After the shot, O₁ and O₂ go to the end of the opposite offensive lines while D goes to the end of his line.

32 ENDLINE AND POST RUNS

Passing	Penalty Area	4 Players	1 Ball

Movement
Without the Ball

CONTRIBUTOR: Robert Seddon, University of Pennsylvania, Philadelphia, Pa. 19174

Formation: X_1 and X_2 are about fifteen yards apart just outside the penalty area. X_3 and X_4 are about ten yards closer to goal than X_2 and X_1 respectively.

X-Field player
Pass_ _ _ _ _⟶
Run_____⟶
Ball .

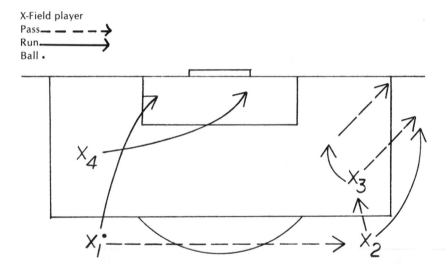

Procedure: X_1 starts the drill with a square pass to X_2. X_2 passes the ball to X_3. X_3 has options of a one touch pass to X_2 cutting by him on the outside or turning in and passing the ball to X_2 on the endline. From the endline, X_2 cuts the ball to X_4 at the near post or X_1 at the far post. X_1 and X_4 have timed their runs to arrive at the posts at the same time as the ball.

After a specified number of turns, players rotate positions in a counter clockwise direction. The drill is also performed on the opposite side.

33 ENDURANCE JUMP

Goalkeeping   Any Area   Goalkeeper   3 Balls

Fitness

Formation: A ball is placed on the ground. A goalkeeper stands to one side of the ball. A feeder faces the goalkeeper 2 yards away.

F-Feeder
G-Goalkeeper
Jump
Pass
Ball •

Procedure: The feeder tosses a ball to the goalkeeper; first to one side of the ball on the ground, then to the other. The goalkeeper jumps over the ball to field the serves. The drill proceeds for a prescribed period of time i.e. one, two, three minutes.

34 ENDURANCE MARKING

Fitness   Perimeter of Field   2-24 Players   1 Ball
                                                                  for every
                                                                  pair of
                                                                  players

---

Formation: Players, in pairs, face each other on the endline of the soccer field.

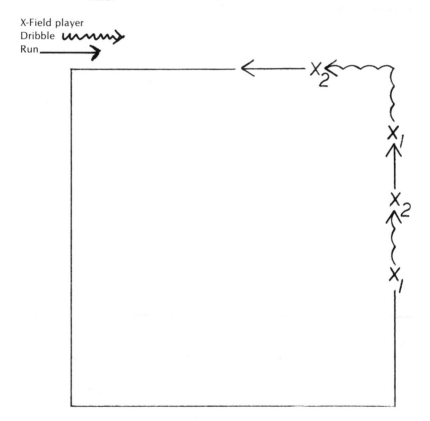

X-Field player
Dribble
Run

Procedure: At a signal, one player in each pair dribbles in a counter clockwise direction while the other player runs backwards, passively marking his partner. Goalkeepers roll or dribble the ball with the hand while their partner marks.

After a complete circuit around the field, dribblers play defense and markers dribble.

35 EXPLODE

Fitness 10 yd. Area 1 Player 1 Ball

1 Cone

Formation: A cone is placed about five yards from X₁.

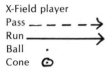

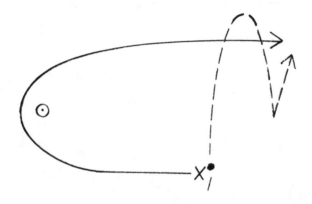

Procedure: X₁ throws the ball about ten feet in the air and, before it bounces a second time, sprints around the cone, controls the ball and moves off with it quickly.

36 FAST BREAK

Movement	½ Field	4 or More Players	3 Balls
With/Without			
the Ball		Goalkeeper(s)	Goal

CONTRIBUTOR: Ed Athey, Washington College, Chestertown, Maryland, 21620

Formation: Four offensive players line up against three defensive players at midfield. A second and third offensive line may set up behind the first line, while a second and third defensive line may wait at the side of the field.

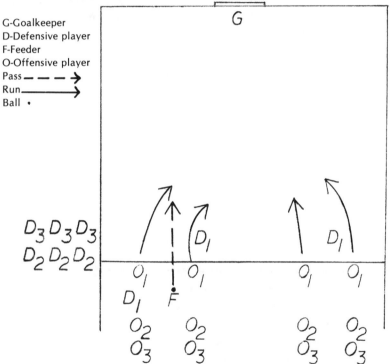

G-Goalkeeper
D-Defensive player
F-Feeder
O-Offensive player
Pass — — — →
Run ——————→
Ball •

Procedure: Feeder passes to offensive player in area vacated by a defensive player who is caught upfield out of his defensive position. The job of the offensive players is to exploit the situation and attack the four on two situations. Defenders attempt to compensate against being outmanned as best they can. Play continues until a goal is scored, the defense gains possession and clears, or the ball goes out of bounds. After play is complete the waiting players assume positions to continue the drill.

37 FIRST TIME SHOOTING

Shooting	Penalty Area	5 Players	6 Balls
		Goalkeeper	1 Cone
Fitness			Goal
Goalkeeping			

Formation: A cone is placed eighteen yards out from the center of the goal. One player stands about three yards behind the cone, a second player is positioned about ten yards to the right of the cone with 3 balls, and a third player is about ten yards to the left of the cone also with 3 balls. A goalkeeper is in goal. Two retrievers stand behind the goal.

F-Feeder
G-Goalkeeper
O-Offensive player
R-Retriever
Pass _ _ _ _ _ _ →
Run _ _ _ _ _ _ →
Shot _ _ _ _ _ _ →
Cone ⊙

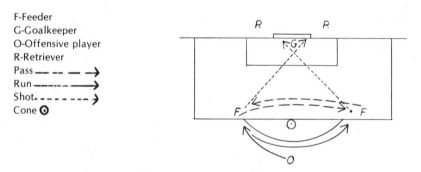

Procedure: The feeder on the right side passes the ball past the cone between the goal and the cone. The shooter makes a run to the left of the cone and shoots first time. The shooter then runs in a semi-circle behind and then to the right of the cone to meet a pass from the feeder on the left side of the cone and again shoots first time.

Retrievers and the goalkeeper return balls to feeders. The drill continues for one minute after which each player, except the goalkeeper, moves to the next position in a clockwise direction.

Variation: 1. The shooter may remain in his position for longer than one minute.
2. Feeders may serve high balls for head shots.
3. A competitive element may be added by counting the number of scores in the given time period.

38 FIVE A-SIDE KEEP AWAY

Offensive and   ½ Field   10 or More Players   1 Ball
Defensive Techniques

Scrimmage
Vests

Fitness

CONTRIBUTOR: Bob Guelker, Southern Illinois University, Edwardsville, Ill.
62025

Procedure: The drill which is simply a keep away game, is usually conducted with five players on each side in one half of the field. No
goals are used. The drill lasts for ten-twelve minutes at a fast
pace with one and two touch passing restrictions. While this drill
fits the Economy of Training Concept by combining technique,
tactics and fitness, it could be organized to emphasize a specific
aspect of the game. For example, early season training would
emphasize fitness, while tight marking would be emphasized as
the season progresses.

Variation: 1. A "swinger" player who plays with the team in possession of
the ball.
2. To restrict space, play six and seven a-side in same area.
3. To sharpen passing and marking, play four a-side in
30 yd. × 30 yd. area.
4. For a light workout, play eight or nine a-side, with loose marking, on three-fourths of the field.

39 FIVE VS FIVE VS FIVE

Offensive and	Full Field	15 Players	1 Ball
Defensive Techniques			
		2 Goalkeepers	

CONTRIBUTOR: Bud Lewis, Wilmington College, Wilmington, Ohio, 45177

Formation: There are three teams (X_1, X_2, X_3) of five players each. Two teams are spread out in one half field and a third team is in the other half field. A goalkeeper defends each goal.

G-Goalkeeper
X-Field player
Ball •

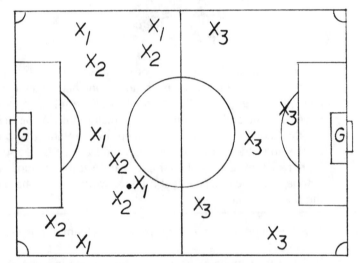

Procedure: The X_1 team starts the drill by attacking the goal defended by the X_2 team. If X_2 wins the ball, they must get it across midfield while X_1 tries to prevent this and get back on attack. Should X_2 succeed in getting the ball over mid-field, they attack the goal defended by the X_3 team. Play continues in the same fashion with a different team trying to cross midfield each time. If one team scores, they maintain possession and restart the drill attacking the opposite goal.

Variation: Different size squads can be used to emphasize different situations. E.G., 1 vs 1 vs 1, 2 vs 2 vs 2, etc.

40 FOLLOW THE LEADER

Dribbling   Any Area   6 Players   6 Balls

Formation: The players, each with a ball, are in a line.

X-Field player
Dribble 〰〰〰〰〰▷
Run ————▷
Ball •

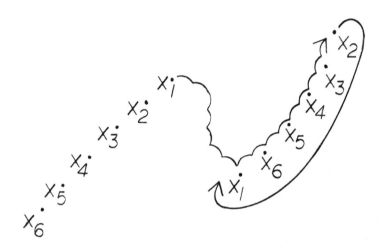

Procedure: The players all dribble, following X_1, who is the leader. At a given signal, all the players stop their ball with a sole trap and move ahead to the next ball. X_1 runs to the rear of the line for the remaining ball. The new leader, X_2, now continues the dribbling until the next signal when another change is made. This procedure continues until X_1 is back in his original position.

41 FOLLOW THE LEADER SKILLS

Offensive and   Open Space   2-24 Players   1 Ball
Defensive Techniques   for every
                                                             player

---

Formation: Players pair off. One player in each pair is designated leader.

X-Field player

$$X_2 \quad X_1$$

Procedure: The leader of each pair performs various skills and moves while the follower imitates. Examples of skills and moves include juggling, dribbling, feinting, faking, sprinting with the ball, passing and shooting at targets.

42 FOLLOW THE PASS

Passing ½ Field 3 or More Players 1 Ball
per group
Goalkeeper
Movement Without the Ball
Shooting

Formation: Three lines of players, facing the goal, are at mid-field. The three lines are about fifteen yards apart with the center line at the middle of the center circle. A goalkeeper is in goal.

G-Goalkeeper
X-Field player
Pass _ _ _ →
Run_____→
Shot.. ... --→
Ball .

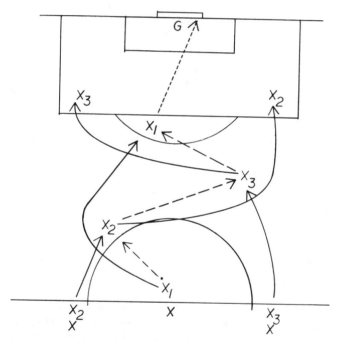

Procedure: X_1 starts the drill by passing diagonally forward to X_2 (the first pass may be made in either direction). X_2 runs to receive the ball and makes a first time pass diagonally forward to X_3 who has run forward to receive it. X_3 also makes a first time pass to X_1 whose run should have him receive the ball just outside the penalty area. X_1 takes a first time shot. X_2 and X_3 continue their runs and are ready for rebound shots. All players follow their passes by running behind the player they pass to (an overlap). The players switch lines after each shot.

63

43 FORWARDS MOVING

Offensive and   Full Field   16 Players   1 Ball
Defensive Techniques

2 Goalkeepers   2 Goals

Formation: Eight players on each team are divided so that there is a four on four situation in each half-field with goalkeepers. Four players on each team are designated forwards and work against the four players on the other team that are designated backs.

G-Goalkeeper
X-Field player
Pass— — —⟩
Run———⟩
Ball •

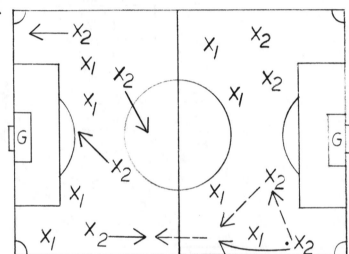

Procedure: Players must remain in their half-field only, but may pass the ball anywhere. When a team's backs have possession, their forwards in the other half of the field must be constantly moving off the ball to get free or create openings for other forwards. When the forwards have possession, they continue attacking until ball possession is lost or a shot on goal is taken. The defenders pressure to regain possession. Throw-ins, corner kicks, goal kicks and free kicks are taken as usual. After a goal is scored, a goal kick is taken. The goalie must throw the ball to one of his backs after a goal save.

The drill can be practiced without restrictions or with specific restrictions as the coach desires.

44 FOUR CORNER PASS

Passing ½ Field 8-24 Players 4 Balls

Dribble

Formation: Players form lines at each corner of half of the field. A ball is at the feet of the first player in each line.

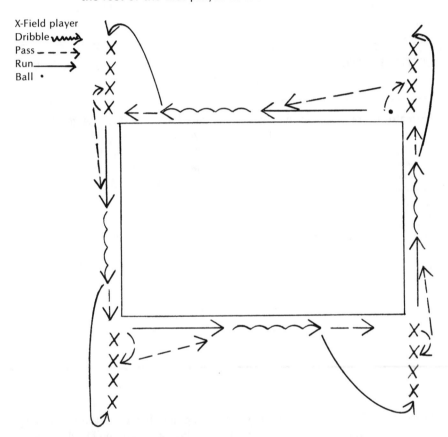

Procedure: The first player in each line passes the ball to the second player in line and makes a run in a counter clockwise direction. The second player in line passes forward to the first player who has made the run. The first player dribbles to the next line, passes the first man in that line and goes to the end of the line. The procedure is repeated starting with the man who received the ball in each line and continues for a prescribed time period.

45 FOUR CORNER-SHOOT

Shooting	30 yd. Area in Front of Goal	5 or More Players	6 Balls
		Goalkeepers	Goal

Goalkeeping
Passing

CONTRIBUTOR: Ronald W. Shewgraft, North Adams State College, North Adams, Massachussetts 01247

Formation: Players form five lines as indicated in the diagram. A goalkeeper is in the goal. Balls are at line A—the starting line.

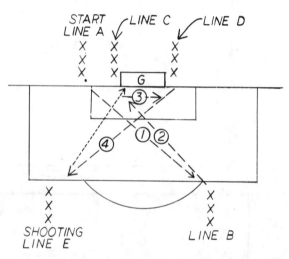

Procedure: The first player on line A (starting line) passes to the first player on line B who passes to line C, who passes to line D, who passes to the first player on line E, the shooting line. This player shoots first time. Players sprint to the end of the line to which they passed the ball. The shooter sprints to the end of the starting line.

Variation:
1. The drill can be done from either side.
2. The angle and distance of the shot can be adjusted.
3. Players can be limited to one touch in passing.

46 FOUR vs FOUR PRESSURE

Offensive and   Penalty Area   12 Players   8 Balls
Defensive Techniques

                                                  Goalkeeper

Goalkeeping
Shooting

CONTRIBUTOR: William G. Rogers, Babson College, Babson Park
Massachusetts 02157

Formation: Four attackers compete against four defenders and a
goalkeeper in the penalty area. Two players, with a supply of
balls, are located at the sides of the area, and serve as feeders.
Two other players are outside the top of the area.

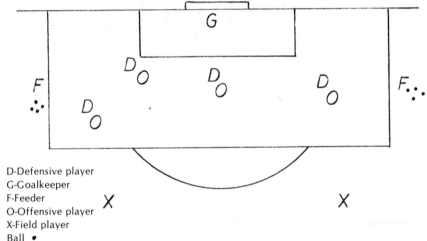

D-Defensive player
G-Goalkeeper
F-Feeder
O-Offensive player
X-Field player
Ball •

Procedure: One of the feeders crosses or passes a ball into the area and the
players compete against each other until a goal is scored or the
ball is cleared out of the area. The players at the top of the area
shoot or pass balls cleared their way back into the area. Other-
wise, one of the feeders will make another cross or pass.

All players are rotated after a specified period of time.

Variation: 1. Change the number of players in the area.
2. Use a *strict* man to man defense.
3. Vary the types of crosses and passes.

47 FULL FIELD ATTACK vs DEFENSE

Offensive and   Full Field   20 Players   1 or More Balls
Defensive Techniques

                              2 Goalkeepers   4 Cones

                              2 Goals

Formation: A regulation field is divided into three tactical areas (defense, mid-field and attack) by cones. Two full teams are positioned according to the tactics being emphasized and system used.

D-Defensive player
F-Feeder
G-Goalkeeper
O-Offensive player
Pass — — — — →
Ball •
Cone ◎

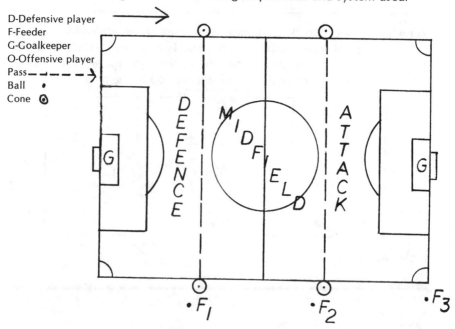

Procedure: F_1 passes the ball to the goalkeeper anywhere in the goal area. The ball must get to the mid-field area in a maximun of two touches.

F_2 passes the ball to any defender anywhere in the mid-field area. The ball must get to the attack area in a maximum of three touches.

F_3 passes the ball to a mid-fielder or attacker anywhere in the mid-field or attack area. Play continues until an attempt on goal is made or the defense gains possession. Specific groups or two full teams can be used. Work in one area at least ten times before moving to another area. Defense can be passive at first with pressure increased as desired.

48 FUNCTIONAL TRAINING FOR FORWARDS

Movement With/ Without the Ball	½ Field	7 Players	3 Balls
		Goalkeeper	Goal
Passing Shooting			

CONTRIBUTOR: Tim Schum, State University of New York at Binghampton, N.Y. 13901

Formation: An outside mid-fielder M₁ has a supply of balls. M₁ starts the drill. Additional offensive, defensive and mid-field players are positioned as shown in the diagram. A goalkeeper is in goal.

G-Goalkeeper
D-Defensive player
M-Midfield players
O-Offensive player
Dribble
Pass
Run
Ball •

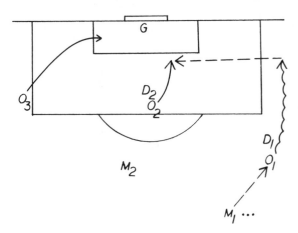

Procedure: M_1 passes to O_1 (given room by D_1). O_1 goes one vs one with D_1 with objective of moving to the endline to make a crossing pass to O_2 who has moved to near post, or O_3 who is breaking to far post, or to M_2 who moves to the eighteen yard line. As soon as the play is over O_1 moves back to receive another pass from M_1. Play continues for two minutes. Play then can be developed on the other side of the field.

Variation: 1. M_1 passes to M_2 who passes to O_1 who has moved behind D_1 (give and go pass).
2. M_1 chips the ball over D_1 to O_1 to start the play.
3. Add defensive man (sweeper) behind D_2 to pick up open offensive players.

69

49 GET GOALSIDE

Defensive Techniques   30 yd. by 30 yd. Area   2 Players   1 Ball

                                                       2 Cones

Fitness

Formation: Two players are next to each other about thirty yards from a three yard wide goal. O, with a ball, stands facing the goal. D is kneeling and facing the opposite direction.

D-Defensive player
O-Offensive player
Dribble
Run
Ball   •
Cone

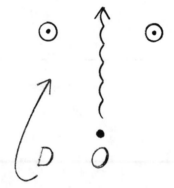

Procedure: O sprint dribbles on goal. D immediately jumps from his kneeling position, turns and sprints to get goalside before O can dribble the ball through the goal.

50 GET TO THE BALL

Shooting　　½ Field　　　　16 Players　　12 Balls

　　　　　　　　　　　　　　　Goalkeeper　　Goal

Defensive Techniques
Goalkeeping

Formation: A feeder stand forty yards from the goal with a supply of balls. A line of offensive players is to one side of the feeder and a line of defensive players is on the other side. A goalkeeper is in goal.

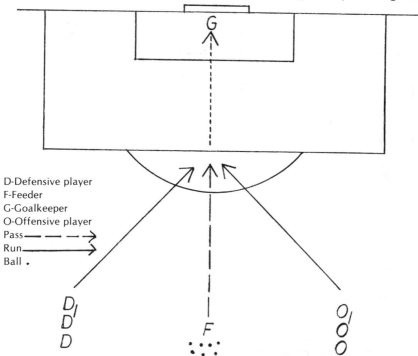

D-Defensive player
F-Feeder
G-Goalkeeper
O-Offensive player
Pass — — — →
Run ————→
Ball .

Procedure: As the feeder passes the ball forward toward the eighteen yard line, the offensive player O_1 and the defensive player D_1 sprint to the ball. The offensive player must get to the ball and shoot on goal before the ball enters the penalty area. The defensive player sprints to defend. O_1 and D_1 switch lines after playing the ball.

Variation: Only the offensive line of players is formed. This puts extra emphasis on sprinting and shooting.

51 GIVE AND GO

Passing   10 yd. by 20 yd. Area   8 Players   1 Ball

Formation: Three players spread out along each side of the area and are available to assist the attacker beat the defender.

D-Defensive player
O-Offensive player
X-Field player
Ball •

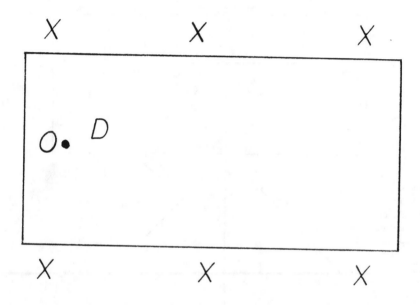

Procedure: O looks for give and go (wall pass) opportunities with any of the outside players (X) as he tries to beat D and reach the other end of the area. If successful, he turns and attacks D in the other direction. If unsuccessful, he tries again. Play should be continuous.

Rotate the players after a set time period.

52 GOALKEEPER DISTANCE THROW

Throwing　　　Length of Soccer Field　　　2 Goalkeepers　　　1 Ball

Formation: Two goalkeepers face each other forty yards apart with the center stripe of the field between them.

G-Goalkeeper

Pass — — — →

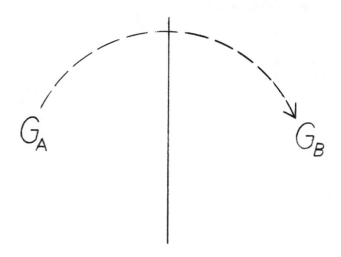

Procedure: Goalkeeper A throws the ball to goalkeeper B. If goalkeeper B fumbles, he moves back ten yards. Goalkeeper B throws to goalkeeper A. Each player attempts to drive the other over the end line of the field. If the ball goes over the receiver's head, it is returned to the point where it first touched the ground.

Variation: Goalkeepers punt or drop kick.

53 GOALKEEPER DIVING

Goalkeeping   10 yd. by 20 yd. Area   4 Players   2-6 Balls

Goalkeeper

Passing

Formation: A goalkeeper is surrounded by four field players. Two of the field players have a ball at their feet. The goalkeeper faces the players with the balls.

G-Goalkeeper
X-Field player
Pass __ __ __ →
Run ——————→
Ball •

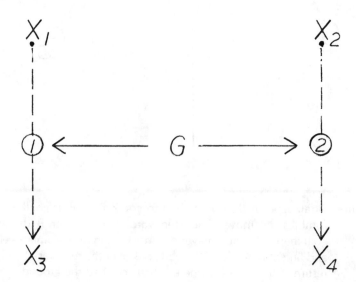

Procedure: Player X_1 passes ball to X_3 while the goalkeeper attempts to dive and save. The goalkeeper recovers and X_2 passes to X_4 as the goalkeeper attempts to dive and make save. The goalkeeper turns to face X_3 and X_4 and the activity continues. The drill continues for thirty, sixty or ninety seconds.

74

54 GOALKEEPER JUDGEMENT

Goalkeeping   ½ Field   12 Players   6 Balls

Goalkeeper

Formation: Two lines of field players form at mid-field. A feeder is between the two lines with a supply of balls. A goalkeeper is in goal.

F-Feeder   Pass — — — →
G-Goalkeeper   Run ——————→
O-Offensive players Ball •

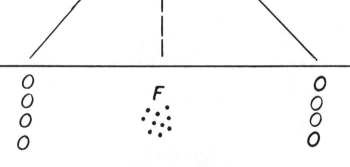

Procedure: Two offensive players sprint toward the goal from mid-field. The feeder sends high and ground balls to an area between the offensive players and the goalkeeper. Serves are timed to make the situation challenging. The goalkeeper may attempt to field the ball before the offensive players arrive.

55 GOALKEEPER PRESSURE

Goalkeeping   10 yd. by 20 yd. Area   2 Players   2 Balls

Goalkeeper

Formation: A goalkeeper is in the middle of the area with two players, each
with a ball, at opposite ends of the area.

G-Goalkeeper
X-Field player
Shot - - - - - →
Ball •

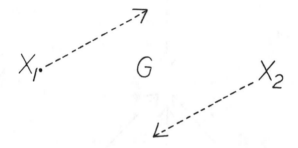

Procedure: X_1 shoots at the goalkeeper. After the goalkeeper attempts to
save the ball, he immediately turns and attempts to save a shot
taken by X_2. The shooters should vary the angle, height and
power of the shot, but not so that it is impossible for the
goalkeeper to make the saves.

56 GOALKEEPER REACTION

Goalkeeping   Kickboard or Wall   2 Goalkeepers   1 Ball

Fitness

Procedure: Standing about six feet from the board or wall, the goalkeeper makes continual above the head volleys against the board with a ball. He holds his elbows above shoulder height and uses finger tips only.

Facing the wall at varying distances, the goalkeeper catches balls rebounding from the wall. A second goalkeeper throws the ball from behind at various heights and speeds.

Facing the second goalkeeper, the goalkeeper, with his back to the wall, turns to catch balls rebounding off the wall after they are thrown over his shoulder or side.

The goalkeeper punts or volley kicks the ball against the wall and catches the rebound.

The distance from the wall and speed of the passes will vary as skill increases.

57 HALF VOLLEY PRACTICE

Shooting   25 yd. Area in   2-12 Players   12 Balls
                    Front of A Goal
                                            Goalkeeper

Formation: Players form a straight line twenty-five yards in front of a goal. Each player holds a ball in his hands. A goalkeeper is in the goal.

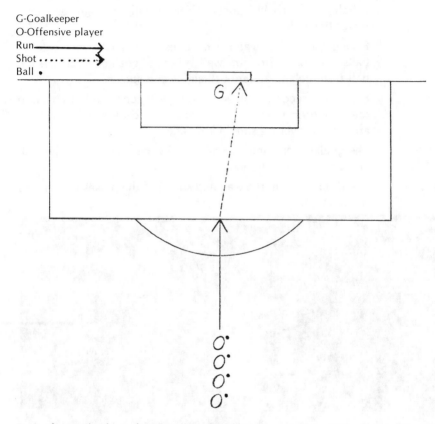

G-Goalkeeper
O-Offensive player
Run
Shot
Ball •

Procedure: The first player in line runs from twenty-five yards out and drops the ball to the ground on the eighteen yard line and takes a shot on the half-volley. Shooters retrieve the ball if they miss the goal.

Variation: Kick the ball before it touches the ground (volley).

58 HEAD WITH DIRECTION

Heading   Any Area   2 Players   1 Ball

Fitness

Formation: One player with a ball in his hand stands five yards from another player.

X-Field player
Pass — — — →
Run ——————→
Ball •

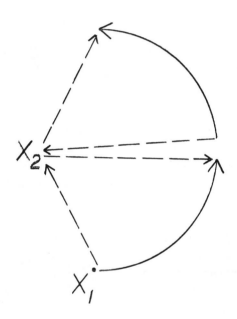

Procedure: X_1, with the ball, tosses the ball to X_2, who heads it back to X_1, who has started to run around X_2 in a counter clockwise direction. X_1 then heads the ball back to X_2, who turns to meet and return the ball. This process continues for one minute in each direction. After two minutes players exchange roles.

59 HEADING OVER OPPONENT

Heading   10 yd. Area   3 Players   1 Ball

Formation: The defender stands in front of the header and between the header and the feeder who is ten yards away with a ball.

D-Defensive player
F-Feeder
O-Offensive player
Pass — — — →
Ball •

Procedure: The following progression is recommended:

F throws to O, who jump heads back to F over D who offers no resistance.

As in #1, with D giving passive resistance.

As in #1, with D giving active resistance.

F throws in air over O and D, who both fight to head the ball. The players will rotate positions after a specified time period.

60 HEADS UP

Dribbling   Center Circle   6 or More Players   1 Ball
                                                    per Player

---

Formation: The players, each with a soccer ball, spread out within the center circle or similar size area. The coach moves slowly within the area.

C-Coach
X-Field player
Dribble ⌇⌇⌇⌇
Ball •

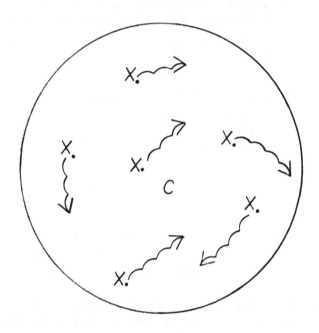

Procedure: The players dribble within the circle. They are instructed to dribble with their heads up and to avoid contact with the other players by changing direction and speed.

The coach periodically holds his hand up signalling a number (zero for closed fist and one through five for each raised finger). The players are to shout out the number.

61 HIGH, WIDE AND FAR

Heading   ¼ Field   5 or More Players   8 Balls

                                                        1 Goal

Fitness

CONTRIBUTOR: John Boles, Temple University, Philadelphia, Pennsylvania
             19122,

Formation: One player stands in the goal on the goal line. Four players, each
with two balls, are located at various spots six to twelve yards
outside the penalty area. Other players may serve as retrievers.

D-Defensive player
F-Feeder
R-Retriever
Ball •

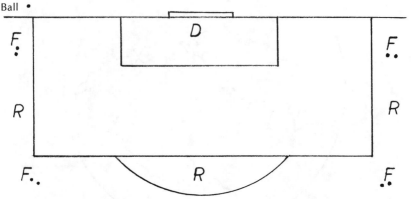

Procedure: D runs to head eight balls being served, one at a time, by the
feeders. D tries to clear each ball outside the eighteen and
returns to the goal line after heading each ball. The feeders
alternate short and long passes. After eight passes the players
rotate to a new position.

62 HIT AND RUN

Fitness 20 yd. by 20 yd. Area 2 Players None

Formation: X_1 stands on a line facing another line twenty yards away. His partner, X_2, is about a foot away facing him.

X-Field player
Run ———→

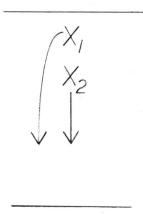

Procedure: X_2 must touch X_1 three times. He may tag him anywhere and in any pattern he choses. After the third touch, X_2 sprints to the furthest line and is chased by X_1. If X_2 gets to the line before X_1 tags him, X_1 must carry X_2 back to the start. If X_1 does tag X_2 before the line, he is carried back to start by X_2.
Repeat the drill with X_1 now making the three touches.

63 HUSTLE TO THE BALL

Fitness   Goal Area   3 Players   4 Balls

Passing
Receiving

Formation: A player positions himself between the two uprights of the goal. Two other players face the goal six yards in front of each post (each of these players have a ball at their feet).

X-Field player

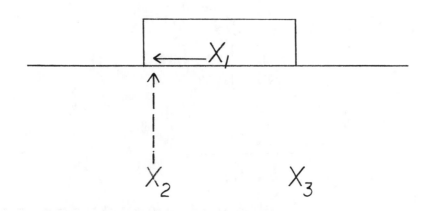

Procedure: X₂ passes the ball to the near post. X₁ runs to meet the ball and return it to X₂. X₁ recovers and runs to the other post to receive the ball being pased by X₃. X₁ returns the ball to X₃ and runs to the other post, etc. X₁ continues in this manner for a prescribed time (usually one or two minutes), after which the players rotate clockwise and assume new roles.

Variation: A goalkeeper is in the goal and moves from one side to the other to:
1. Catch ground balls   4. Punch high balls
2. Catch air balls   5. Dive for shots
3. Tip balls over top

64 IMMEDIATE CHASE

Defensive Techniques   30 yd. by 30 yd. Area   2 Players   2 Balls

3 Cones

Dribbling
Fitness

Formation: X_2 faces a three yard wide goal thirty yards away. X_1 stands to the side of this goal facing a cone ten yards to the side of X_2. Each player has a ball.

X-Field player
Dribble 〰〰〰〰➤
Run ──────➤
Ball •
Cone ◉

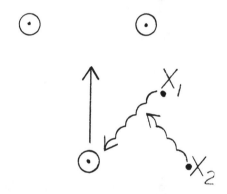

Procedure: X_1 dribbles to the cone. As soon as X_1 reaches the cone, X_2 sprint dribbles to the goal while X_1 must make an immediate turn and recovery run in an attempt to get goal-side before X_2 can dribble through the goal.

65 IN AND OUT

Passing   10 yd. by 10 yd. Area   4 Players   1 Ball

Formation: Four players, with one ball, are in an area about 10 yards from each other.

X-Field player
Ball •

X_4 X_3

Procedure: The four players one touch pass to each other. Starting wide, they pass slowly, but as they move toward each other, the passing is faster. The players move in and out together, continually passing.

66 JUMP HEADING

Fitness   Any Area   3 or More Players   2 Balls
                                                          per Group
Heading

Formation: One player (X₁) stands between two other players who are each holding a ball at jump height. X₁ allows enough room to turn and jump comfortably.

X-Field Player
Ball •

$$X. \qquad X_1 \qquad .X$$

Procedure: The two outside players hold the balls at jump height while X₁ jumps and alternately heads each ball, turning after each head. After thirty seconds, a new player becomes the middle player.

67 KEEPAWAY

Passing   15 yd. by 20 yd. Area   10 Players   1 Ball

4 Cones

Defensive Techniques   4 Scrimmage
                                                         Vests

---

CONTRIBUTOR: John Rennie, Duke University, Durham,
North Carolina 27706

Formation: One offensive player is in the middle of the area, with five team-mates spread around the area's boundaries. Four defenders, wearing vests, are located anywhere in the area.

D-Defensive Player
O-Offensive Player
Ball   •
Cone   ◉

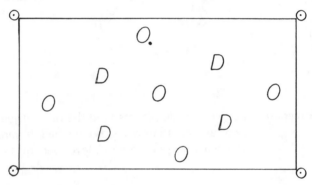

Procedure: The six offensive players play two touch keepaway against the four defenders. If a defender wins the ball, it is immediately returned to the attackers. Every two minutes, four offensive players change positions with the defenders, and a new offensive player goes into the middle.

The object is for the offensive players to make as many consecutive passes as possible. The middle offensive player counts the passes, while a defender counts the number of offensive breakdowns in each time period. Each group tries to beat the best number.

Variation: 1. Vary area size
2. Play one touch
3. Add another offensive player
4. Vary defensive tempo

88

68 KEEPER COURAGE

Goalkeeping   Goal Area   1 Player   10 Balls

Goalkeeper

Formation: Ten balls are placed one yard apart along the six yard line. A goalkeeper is stretched out on the ground prepared to take the impact of the first ball when kicked at his body by an offensive player.

G-Goalkeeper
O-Offensive Player
Ball •

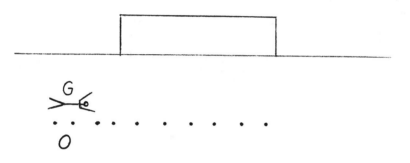

Procedure: An offensive player kicks 10 balls in succession at the upper body of the goalkeeper. After attempting to field each ball the goalkeeper scoots along the ground attempting to get into position to field the next ball.

69 LEAVE IT

Passing   ½ Field   9 or More Players   3 Balls

                                Goalkeeper   1 Goal

Movement Without the Ball
Shooting

Formation: Three lines of players are about twenty yards outside the penalty area in basic attack positions.

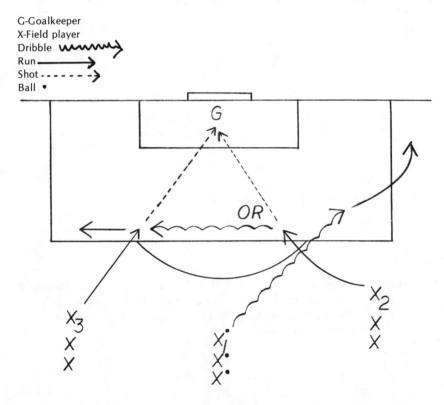

G-Goalkeeper
X-Field player
Dribble
Run
Shot
Ball •

Procedure: X_1 dribbles towards and past X_2 who has timed his run to arrive at a particular point just behind X_1. X_1 leaves (or back heels) the ball for X_2 and continues a run off the ball. X_2 may shoot or dribble across the area to leave the ball for X_3 who shoots.

70 MAN ON

Passing ½ Field 11 Players 8 Balls

Goalkeeper

Communication
Shooting
Turning

CONTRIBUTOR: Howard Goldman, Marist College, Poughkeepsie, New York 12601

Formation: There are three lines of players; one alongside the goal, one just outside the restraining circle, and one inside the center circle. A goalkeeper is in goal, and a supply of balls is at mid-field.

D-Defensive Player
G-Goalkeeper
O-Offensive player
Pass -- --- — — →
Run ————————→
Ball

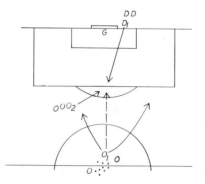

Procedure: O_1, at mid-field, starts the drill by passing to O_2, who has moved to the center of the restraining circle. D_1 moves to top of penalty area to act as defender. O_1 runs toward O_2 and, depending on position of D_1 gives verbal assistance to O_2 (E.G., man on, turn). D_1 can play tight on O_2 or look to stop pass to O_1. The object is for O_2 to turn and shoot or to pass to O_1 who shoots. Shots are outside the eighteen with the emphasis on quick decisions, passes and shots.

Variation: 1. One touch only
2. Vary passes to O_2
3. Allow defensive player early start
4. Add second defender

71 MIDFIELDER PRESSURE

Offensive and　　　　　10 yd. by 5 yd. Area　　3 Players　　2 Balls
Defensive Techniques

CONTRIBUTOR: Gary J. Hindley, Trenton State College, Trenton, New Jersey 08625

Formation: One player is in the center of the area with two other players, acting as feeders, at opposite ends of the area.

F-Feeder
X-Field Player
Ball •

$$F_1 \bullet \qquad X \qquad \bullet F_2$$

Procedure: Each feeder alternates passing various types of ball for X. After X completes the specified technique while facing one feeder, he then turns and completes a different skill in the other direction. X continues this procedure for thirty seconds to one minute. Players then rotate positions until each player has been in the middle after which new techniques are practiced.

Variation: The following are four combinations that can be used:
1. F_1 rolls ball - X makes a one touch return.
   F_2 passes ball in air - X chest traps and makes a volley return.
2. F_1 passes ball in air - X makes a volley pass back.
   F_2 passes ball in air - X heads the ball back.
3. F_1 rolls ball - X makes a two touch return
   F_2 passes ball in air - X thigh traps and makes a half volley return.
4. F_1 passes ball in air - X jumps to head ball back.
   F_2 passes ball in air - X instep traps and returns ball with foot pass.

72 MINI GAME

| *Offensive and Defensive Techniques* | 30 yd. by 30 yd. Area | 8 Players | 1 Ball |
| | | 2 Goalkeepers | 4 Cones |

Fitness

CONTRIBUTOR: Will Myers, William Paterson College, Wayne, New Jersey 07470

Formation: Four players (X_1) play against four others (X_2) in a small field. Two cones, three yards apart, are used for each goal (If goalkeepers are used, the cones are eight yards apart). The goals are thirty yards apart.

G-Goalkeeper
X-Field player
Ball •
Cone ⊙

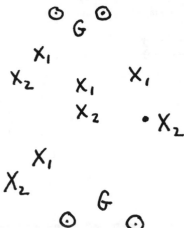

Procedure: The four vs four game begins with a drop ball in the center of the area. The game, played with or without goalkeepers, lasts for ten minutes. There are no boundaries, however, goals may only be scored from the front. Play is continuous.

Variation: 1. Play with a two touch restriction
2. Play with a one touch restriction.
3. Play with a restriction that the ball must be kept below the waist.
4. Play strict man to man defense (no switching allowed).
5. Several games can be played simultaneously with specific teams rotating to another opponent after each time period.

73 MOBILITY

Movement With/Without   20 yd. by 40 yd.   7 Players   6 Balls
the Ball   Area

Defensive Technique
Passing

CONTRIBUTOR: Walter Bahr, The Pennsylvania State Univ., University
Park, Pa. 16802

Formation: Two lines of three players each are about forty yards apart with
a defender in between.

D-Defensive Player
X-Field Player
Pass — — — →
Run ————→

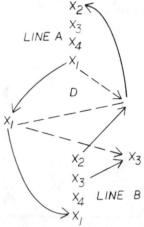

Procedure: X_1, the first player in line A passes to X_2, the first player in line B,
who has made a lateral run to receive the ball. The defensive
player (D) always chases the player with the ball. After passing
to X_2, X_1 makes a run behind the defensive player and receives a
return pass from X_2. X_2 goes to the end of line A. X_1 passes to the
next player in line B, (X_3) who has made a lateral run. X_1 then
goes to the end of line B and the cycle continues in the opposite
direction. The defensive player stays in the center as long as
determined by the coach.

Variation: 1. Require two touch passing.
2. Require one touch passing.
3. Place two defenders between lines A & B.

94

74 NEVER QUIT

Defensive Tecnniques   Penalty Area   1 Player   6 Balls
                                                    a time

Goalkeeping
Fitness

Formation: A feeder with a supply of balls faces a field player or goalkeeper.

F-Feeder
X-Field Player
Pass — — — →
Run ———————→
Ball •

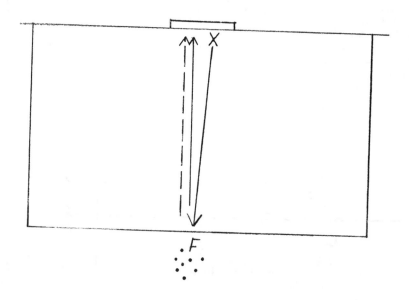

Procedure: X runs up and taps the ball held by the feeder with his hand. After tapping the ball the player sprints to the goal. As the player is recovering the feeder shoots at goal. Field players attempt to legally save the ball while goalkeepers have the advantage of using their hands. The drill continues until the player has attempted 10 saves or until a pre-determined time has elapsed (one or two minutes).

75 OFFENSE TO DEFENSE

Offensive and Defensive Techniques	25 yd. by 50 yd. Area	8-12 Players	4 Balls
		Goalkeeper	2 Goals

Goalkeeping

CONTRIBUTOR: Luis A. Sagastume, U.S. Air Force Academy, Colorado 80840

Formation: Two goals are positioned twenty-five yards apart. Four to six players line up behind the right post of each goal. A goalkeeper is in each goal. Two balls are at each right post.

G-Goalkeeper
X-Field Player
Dribble ∿∿∿∿⟩
Run ⟶
Shot ------⟩
Ball •

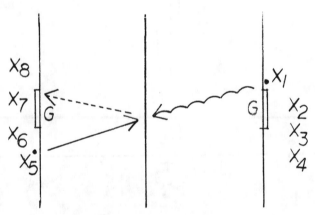

Procedure: Player X_1 attacks and is defended by player X_5. After X_1 either scores or loses possession he becomes a defensive player. X_5 upon winning possession or upon receiving a ball distributed by the goalkeeper becomes an offensive player attacking the opposite goal. Each player completes one offensive and one defensive opportunity. Players go to the end of the opposite line upon completion of offensive and defensive turn.

76 OFFENSIVE BUILD-UP

Movement with/   Full Field   14-22 Players   1 Ball
Without the Ball

                                                2 Goalkeepers

Offensive and
Defensive Techniques

CONTRIBUTOR: Joe Morrone, University of Connecticut, Storrs,
                     Connecticut 06268

Formation: One goalkeeper is in each goal. A full team of backs, mid-
fielders and forwards are spread within the defending half of the
field. The goalkeeper or a back on this team will have a ball.
Three other players, acting as defenders, are also located in the
same half-field.

D-Defensive player
G-Goalkeeper
O-Offensive Player
Ball •

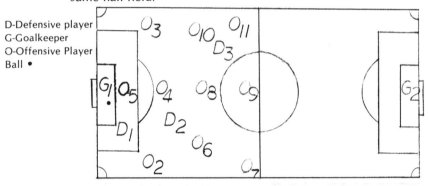

Procedure: The full team attempts to move the ball, against three
defenders, the entire length of the field, get the ball to the
goalkeeper in the offensive penalty area, and then back to the
goalkeeper in the defensive penalty area. The full team players
have a one, two, or three touch restriction, while the three
defenders play unlimited touch should they gain possession of
the ball. The object of the drill is for the team in possession of
the ball to continually change the point of attack and create
situations of numerical superiority (4 vs 3, 3 vs 2, 2 vs 1, etc.).
Each time the full team is successful in moving the ball to the
opposite goalkeeper and back to its own goalkeeper, another
defender is added (up to a full team).

77 ONE ON ONE

Offensive and	½ Field	12 or More Players	3 Balls
Defensive Techniques		Goalkeeper	Goal

Formation: Six defensemen line up behind one post of the goal. Six or more offensive players line up at the center circle. A goalkeeper is in goal.

D-Defensive player
G-Goalkeeper
O-Offensive player
Dribble
Pass
Run
Shot
Ball •

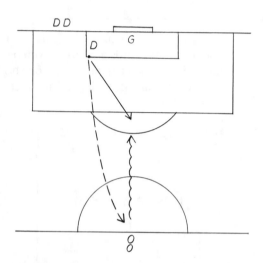

Procedure: A defensive player kicks a goalkick to the center circle. The waiting offensive player receives the ball and dribbles toward the goal. The defensive player who took the goal-kick runs to meet the offensive player and attempts to tackle. If the defensive player is successful, the play ends and the offensive and defensive players go to the end of their respective lines. If the forward is able to maintain possession to the edge of the penalty area, the defensive player releases and the goalkeeper plays the forward one on one.

Variation: 1. Offensive and defensive players exchange lines and roles after each play
2. The defensive player does not release at the edge of the penalty area and both he and the goalkeeper defend.

78 ONE-TWO PASS

Passing   Any Open Space   3 Players   1 Ball

Movement With/
Without the Ball

CONTRIBUTOR: Geza Henni, University of Rhode Island, Kingston,
Rhode Island 02881

Formation: Two players, X₂ and X₃, are about five yards apart on the same
plane. X₁, also five yards away, is directly opposite and facing X₂
who has a ball.

X-Field player
Dribble
Pass
Run
Ball •

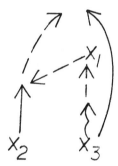

Procedure: X₁ is running backwards or sideways. X₂ dribbles toward X₁, with
X₃ moving parallel to X₂. X₂ pushes the ball to X₁ who first time
passes on a forty-five degree angle to X₃ who is moving forward
to receive the ball. X₃ immediately passes the ball to X₂, who has
made a run past X₁. The players should rotate positions
periodically. The drill should be done to both sides (i.e., X₃ starts
the drill).

Variation: 1. X₂ can shoot on goal or dribble with the ball after receiving
the return pass.
2. X₂ passes the ball back to either X₁ or X₃ who restarts the drill.
3. Add one or more defenders.

79 ONE vs ONE

Containment   10 yd. by 10 yd. Area   2 Players   1 Ball

                                                                4 Cones

Dribbling
Tackling

Formation: D, with a ball, is on one boundary line and O is on the opposite line.

D-Defensive player
O-Offensive Player
Dribble 〰〰〰➤
Pass _ _ _ _ ➔
Run ————➔
Cone ☉
Ball •

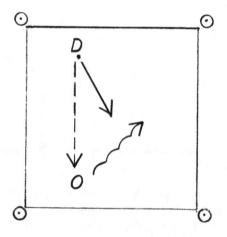

Procedure: D passes to O to start drill. When O receives the ball, D moves to challenge. O tries to get past D to the opposite line. If D gains possession, he goes on attack. When the ball goes out of bounds, the drill is restarted with a pass. The player who succeeds in getting to the line with the ball restarts the drill with a pass to the other player who has returned to the opposite line.

80 ONE vs ONE SCRAMBLE

Dribbling   Full Field   18 Players   9 Balls

Fitness
Passing
Support

CONTRIBUTOR: Steve Griggs, Yale University, New Haven, Connecticut
06520

Formation: Nine attackers, each with a ball. are located anywhere along
one goal line. Nine defenders are located anywhere in the field.

D-Defensive player
O-Offensive player
Dribble 〰〰〰➤
Ball

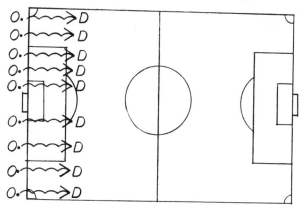

Procedure: The drill starts with all attackers dribbling toward the opposite
goal line. A point is scored for each ball that is pushed (rolled)
across the goal line. Long kicks do not count. The defenders try
to take the balls away from the attackers and push the balls over
the starting goal line. Each ball is "dead" as it is scored, but play
continues with all players supporting their teammates offensive-
ly and defensively until all nine balls are "dead". Passing between teammates should increase as the number of "live" balls
decrease. Balls going over the touch line are put back into play
by a throw in.

After each "game," the teams change positions. Each team is
given three chances to start with the balls with two minutes rest
permitted between games.

81 ONE vs TWO

Containment   10 yd. by 20 yd. Area   3 Players   1 Ball

6 Cones

Dribbling
Tackling

Formation: D_1, in the middle of the area, defends against O, who is on an endline. D_2 starts play at one cone on the same line as O.

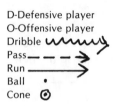

D-Defensive player
O-Offensive player
Dribble
Pass
Run
Ball   •
Cone   ◎

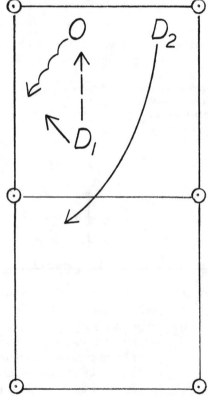

Procedure: D_1 passes to O to start drill. When O receives the ball, D_1 moves to defend against O in the first area. D_2 makes a recovery run after O has made two touches and is ready to defend against O if he beats D_1.

Players rotate positions after a specified time or number of attempts by O.

82 ONE vs THREE

Containment   10 yd. by 30 yd. Area   4 Players   1 Ball

8 Cones

Dribbling
Tackling

Formation: Player O stands on the end line. D_1 is 10 yards away facing O. D_2 is by the cone on the same line as O. D_3 is on the furthest line.

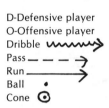

D-Defensive player
O-Offensive player
Dribble
Pass
Run
Ball   •
Cone

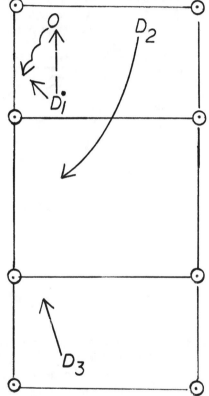

Procedure: O, after receiving pass from D_1, tries to beat him to get into the second area. D_2, waiting until O makes two touches, runs to the second area to challenge O. D_3 remains on the last boundary line until O enters the third area and then moves to challenge him.

The players rotate positions after a specified time or number of attempts by O.

83 OVERLAP

Overlapping   Full Field   3 or More Players   1 Ball

Offensive Techniques   Goalkeeper   Goals
Passing

CONTRIBUTOR: Larry M. Gross, North Carolina State Univ.,
Raleigh, No. Carolina 27650

Formation: A goalkeeper is in the goal, a defender is in front of him, a
striker is upfield by the touch line and a mid-fielder is upfield
closer to the center of the field.

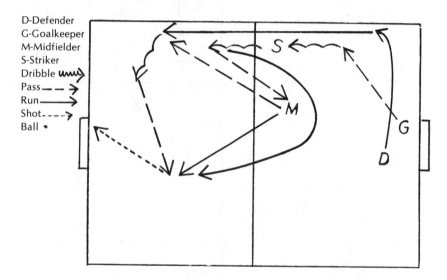

D-Defender
G-Goalkeeper
M-Midfielder
S-Striker
Dribble
Pass
Run
Shot
Ball •

Procedure: The defender runs to receive the ball distributed by the goalkeeper. The defender passes up to the striker who passes to the
mid-fielder. The defender overlaps upfield along the touch line.
The mid-fielder passes upfield to the defender. The mid-fielder
and striker go inside and forward for a cross from the defender.
Another group, or this same group, goes down the field the opposite way following a goalkeeper pass.

Variation: One touch and imaginative passes can be introduced in order to
create different movements.

84 OVERLAP/WARM-UP

Overlapping   Full Field   22 Players   2 Balls

2 Goalkeepers

Offensive Techniques
Passing

CONTRIBUTOR: Jay Martin, Ohio Wesleyan University,
Delaware, Ohio 43015

Formation: Two full teams are located on a full field as follows: A goalkeeper, with a ball, is in each goal; to the right of each goal are four backs; to the left are three forwards; three mid-fielders from each team are to the right and left of the center circle.

B-Back
F-Forward
G-Goalkeeper
MF-Midfielder
Dribble ∿∿∿⟩
Pass — — — ⟩
Run ⟶
Shot - - - - - ⟩
Ball •

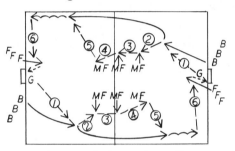

Procedure: The drill starts simultaneously by each goalkeeper rolling a ball (1) to a back who has run to the outside of the penalty area. Each turns the ball upfield and passes (2) to a mid-fielder who runs to meet the pass. The backs sprint up the side line on their overlap run while the mid-fielders one touch pass (3&4) to each other after which a long pass (5) is made to the back. The back dribbles with the ball until he crosses (6) to a forward at the eighteen who shoots on goal. After both shots, the goalies collect the balls and start the drill again.

Backs go to the end of the opposite line, while forwards return to the end of the same line. Mid-fielders can rotate positions on the same side.

Variation: 1. The squads change sides and the ball is brought up the left side of the field.
2. A defender challenges the mid-fielders.
3. Two forwards are in the attack area near each post.
4. A defender challenges the attackers.
5. The mid-fielder passes to the forward who passes it to the back who shoots.

85 PASS AND CHANGE

Passing   15 yd. Square   5 Players   1 Ball

4 Cones

Movement Without the Ball

CONTRIBUTOR: Helmut Werner, Randolph-Macon College,
Ashland, Virginia 23005

Formation: One player, X₅, is in the center of the area, with a player in each of the area's corners. Any one of the corner players has a ball.

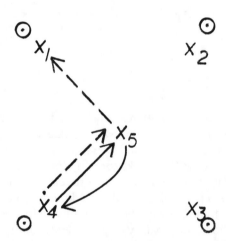

Procedure: The drill may start in any corner. E.G., X₄ starts by passing to X₅. X₅ then passes to X₁, after which X₄ and X₅ exchange positions. The drill continues in the same fashion around the area.

Variation: 1. Two touch
2. One touch
3. Inside of foot
4. Outside of foot

86 PASS AND HEAD

Fitness   ½ Field   3 Players   2 Balls

Heading
Passing

Formation: Two players, X_2 and X_3, each with a ball are on the end line facing X_1 who is five feet away with his back to mid-field.

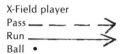

X-Field player
Pass — — — —→
Run ——————→
Ball •

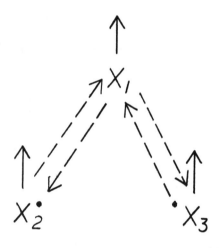

Procedure: X_2 and X_3 alternately throw and pass the ball to X_1. X_1 heads the throw from X_2 and passes the ball from X_3 back to him. X_2 and X_3 are running forward and X_1 backward throughout the drill. When they reach mid-field, they change positions and return to the start performing the same drill. The drill is done twice by each player.

87 PASS AND HELP

Offensive and Defensive Techniques	10 yd. by 10 yd. Area	4 Players	1 Ball
			4 Cones

Formation: This drill is practiced in pairs. One player from each pair is inside the area, while the other two are on opposite endlines.

D-Defensive player
O-Offensive player
Pass — — — →
Run ——→
Ball •
Cone ◉

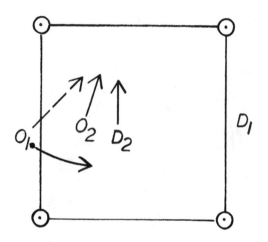

Procedure: O_2 moves to get free to receive a pass from O_1 while D_2 defends. When the pass in is made, O_1 and O_2 try to beat D_2. If successful, or if D_2 interepts, the ball is passed to D_1 who has remained on his line. O_1 returns to his line, as D_1 and D_2 repeat the drill while O_2 defends.

After one minute, the players rotate positions.

88 PASS AND SHOOT

Shooting	½ Field	12 Players	12 Balls
		Goalkeeper	1 Ball

Goalkeeping
Passing

Formation: The players, each with a ball, form two equal lines about thirty yards from goal. The position and role of the feeders will change according to the drill's progressions.

F-Feeder
G-Goalkeeper
X-Field player
Pass — — — →
Run ————→
Ball •

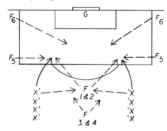

Procedure: Progressions 1 & 2: The feeder is midway between and a few yards ahead of the lines.

1. Each player, in turn and alternating lines, passes on ground to the feeder and runs to shoot, first time, the return ground pass.
2. Repeat #1, with feeder making air passes.

Progressions 3 & 4: The feeder, who has all the balls, stands behind and midway between the lines.

3. The feeder makes passes forward, alternating lines. Each player, in turn, sprints after the pass as soon as he sees the ball. Shots are taken as the ball is reached without making any adjustment in stride.
4. The first player in each line chases each pass. The player who reaches the ball first shoots or goes on attack while the other player defends.

Progressions 5 & 6: Two feeders are on the side lines and corners of the field with all the balls.

5. From the side lines, the feeder passes to players running forward who shoot with leg nearest feeder.
6. With feeders at the corners, the lines move to positions at an angle to the goal. Players take first time shots from a variety of passes.

109

89 PASS BALL FORWARD

Passing   30 yd. by 15 yd. Area   10 Players   1 Ball

Formation: Five players, three attackers and two defenders, are in each half of an area thirty yards long by fifteen yards wide.

D-Defensive player
O-Offensive player
Dribble ⌇⌇⌇➤
Fass ＿ ＿ ＿ ➔
Ball •

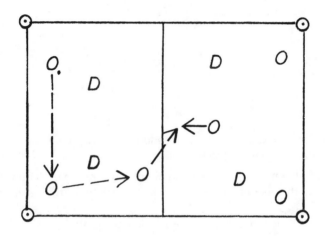

Procedure: The attackers on one side must make three passes; two as a buildup and the third a forward (penetrative) pass which must cross the half-line and be received by one of the other three attackers. The drill is then repeated with the third pass returning to one of the first three attackers, and so on.

Variation: 1. The defenders, at first, offer passive resistance. After awhile they try to take the ball away from the attackers. If successful, the ball is returned to the attackers and the drill starts again.
2. The number of players and size of the area can vary.

90 PASS TO KEEPER

Passing	½ Field	8-12 Players	3 Balls
		Goalkeeper	Goal

Goalkeeping

Formation: Offensive and defensive players line up at mid-field. Feeder separates two lines. A goalkeeper is in the goal.

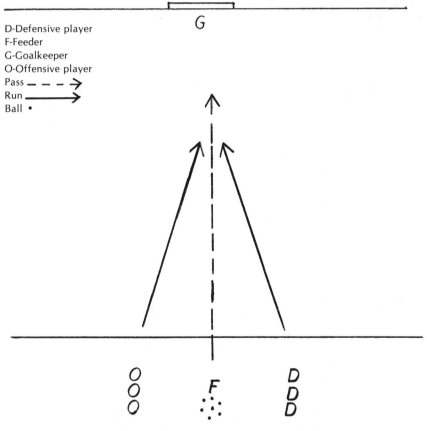

D-Defensive player
F-Feeder
G-Goalkeeper
O-Offensive player
Pass _ _ _ →
Run _____→
Ball •

Procedure: The feeder passes the ball downfield. One offensive and one defensive player sprint to the ball. If the defensive player gains possession he either turns and clears the ball or, if appropriate, passes back to the goalkeeper. If the offensive player gains possession he advances and attempts to shoot on goal.

91 PENALTY KICK COMPETITION

Penalty Kicking   Penalty Area   1 Player   1 Ball

Goalkeeper   Goal

Goalkeeping

Formation: A player is at the penalty mark and a goalkeeper is in goal.

G-Goalkeeper
X-Field player
Ball

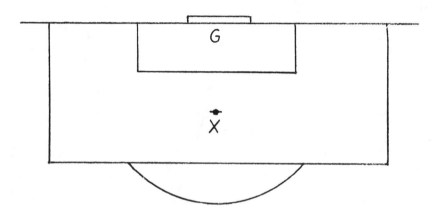

Procedure: The field player takes twelve penalty kicks. Score is kept. The kicker receives one point each time he scores and the goalkeeper receives one point each time he makes a save. In addition, a point is deducted from the kicker's score each time he misses the goal.

Variation: 1. Competitions can be set up in other ways, E.G.,
      A . One vs one with each player taking five shots.
      B . Five vs five with each player taking one shot.
      C . The full team participating with a player eliminated if he misses the goal or the goalie makes the save. Competition continues until one player remains.
  2. Change goalkeepers after every five shots or after every shot.

92 PENETRATE-SUPPORT

Passing   10 yd. by 20 yd. Area   6 Players   1 Ball

Communication
Defensive Techniques

Formation: Two players defend against four other players. Each of the four players must stay along one of the four boundary lines.

D-Defensive player
O-Offensive player
Pass — — — →
Ball •

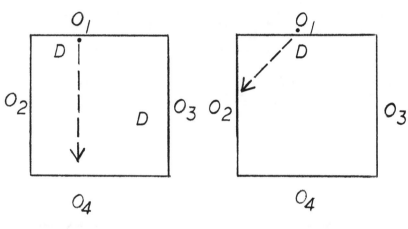

A Successful
Penetrative Pass

Proper Defensive
Support

Procedure: The passers' objective is to make a penetrative pass (O_1 to O_4), while the defenders attempt to prevent such a pass.

93 POST DRILL

Offensive and ½ Field 5 or More Players 6 Balls
Defensive Techniques

Goalkeeper Scrimmage
Vests

CONTRIBUTOR: C. Cliff McGrath, Seattle Pacific University,
Seattle, Washington 98119

Formation: Five lines of players are formed as in the diagram. The first
player in lines D and E stands inside the goal with a hand on the
near goal post. A goalkeeper is in goal. The balls are in the
center circle.

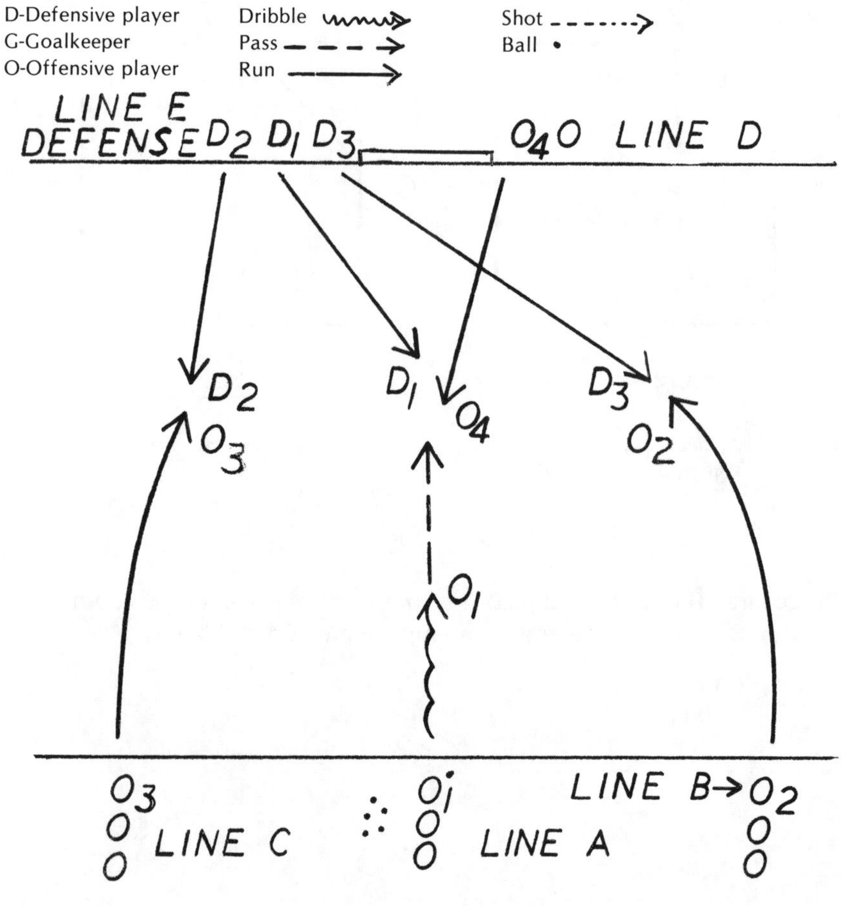

D-Defensive player Dribble ∿∿∿⟶ Shot - - - - - -⟶
G-Goalkeeper Pass — — — ⟶ Ball •
O-Offensive player Run —————⟶

114

Procedure: O_1, the first player in line A, dribbles toward goal. As O_1 makes his approach, O_4, from line D, releases his hand from the post and runs toward him. D_1, from line E, then releases his hand and runs to defend against O_4 or cut off a pass from O_1. O_1 may keep the ball, continue his approach and shoot on goal, or may pass to O_4 and continue moving forward for a possible return pass and a shot on goal.

Meanwhile, O_2 and O_3 from lines B and C, make timed runs into the penalty area for possible passes from O_1 or O_4. Two additional defenders, D_2 and D_3, move to support D_1 as soon as O_4 touches the ball a second time, O_2 or O_3 play the ball, or O_1 dribbles into the penalty area. Any of these situations will create a four vs three plus goalkeeper situation. Play then continues under match conditions until the ball goes out of bounds, a goal is scored or a save is made.

Variation: Score can be kept. The defense scores a point for every offensive thrust they stop. The offense scores two points for every goal scored, and one point for every corner kick.

94 POWER SPRINT

Fitness	½ Field	2 or More Players	None

Formation: The players, in pairs, face each other at mid-field. One player, whose back is to an end line, places his arms on his partner's shoulders.

Procedure: The player facing the end line will sprint to the end line. His partner, while running backwards, offers resistance to the sprinter. The resistance should be enough to make the sprinter work hard but not enough to prevent him from moving. At the end line, the players switch positions and repeat the drill to mid-field.

95 PRESSURE COOKER

Goalkeeping Center Circle or   10 Players   1 Ball
               Similar Size Area

                                      Goalkeeper

Passing
Shooting

CONTRIBUTOR: Owen L. Wright, Elizabethtown College,
                Elizabethtown, Pennsylvania 12022

Formation: Ten players position themselves around the center circle. A
goalkeeper is inside the circle.

G-Goalkeeper
O-Offensive player
Pass — — — — →
Shot - - - - - - - →
Ball •

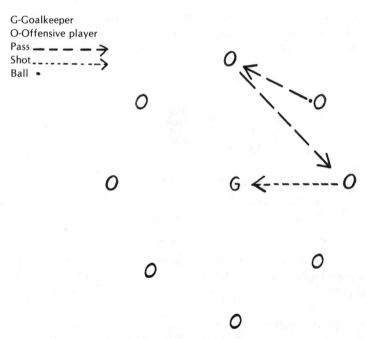

Procedure: Players on the circle keep the ball moving by passing first time.
At any time a player may shoot at the goalkeeper. The goalkeeper must constantly anticipate a shot. After fielding a shot the goalkeeper returns the ball to one of the players on the circle.

96 PRESSURE TURNING

Receiving   10 yd. by 10 yd. Area   4 Players   1 Ball

CONTRIBUTOR: Russ Fager, Rider College, Trenton, New Jersey 08648

Formation: X_2 stands between X_1 and X_3. X_4 stands beside X_2 providing passive pressure.

X-Field player
Pass — — — →
Run ————→

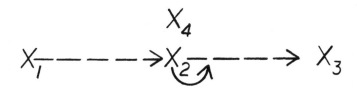

Procedure: X_1 passes to X_2. The pass may be on the ground, or in the air to the thigh, chest, or head. Upon receiving the ball, X_2 turns in one smooth movement and passes to X_3. While X_2 is doing this, X_4 may pressure, even bump, X_2. After the pass to X_3, X_2 is facing X_3 and awaits a return pass. Upon receiving the return pass, X_2 turns and passes to X_1. The drill continues in this fashion for a prescribed period, usually one minute. After one minute, players change positions.

Variation: On the initial pass X_1 may call for a return pass. X_2 in this situation attempts to receive the ball, turn around and return the ball to X_1.

117

97 PREVENT THE HEAD BALL

Goalkeeping   Penalty Area   2-4 Field Players   6 Balls

Goalkeeper

Formation: A line of offensive players forms at the penalty mark. Two feeders, with a supply of balls, are on the 6 yard line. A goalkeeper is positioned in goal.

F-Feeder
G-Goalkeeper
O-Offensive player
Pass — — — →
Run ————→
Ball •

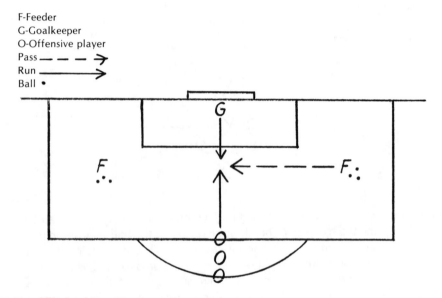

Procedure: The feeders alternately serve balls head high to the center of the six yard line. The goalkeeper comes out to catch or punch. The offensive player charges in as if to head the ball, but only provides passive competition.

Variation: The offensive player attempts to head the ball on goal.

98 PROTECT NEAR POST

Goalkeeping　　　½ Field　　　8 Offensive Players　　　6 Balls

Goalkeeper　　　Goal

Shooting

Formation: Two lines of forwards form thirty yards from a goal. A feeder with a supply of balls is between the lines. A goalkeeper is in goal.

F-Feeder　　　　　　Pass - - - →
G-Goalkeeper　　　　Run ————→
O-Offensive player　Ball •

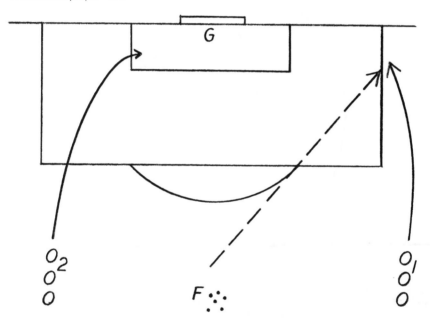

Procedure: The feeder passes to O_1 who has the options of shooting to the near post or crossing to O_2. The goalkeeper must first protect his near post, but also anticipate the possibility that he may have to react to the cross, and intercept, if possible, or prepare for a shot from O_2.

Variation: Add a defensive line at the far post. The defender can back up the goalkeeper and play defense on O_2 if the ball is crossed.

99 PROTECT THE BALL

Dribbling Center Circle 6 or More Players 1 Ball per
Player Less One

Shielding

Formation: The players spread out within the center circle or similar size area. All but one have a ball.

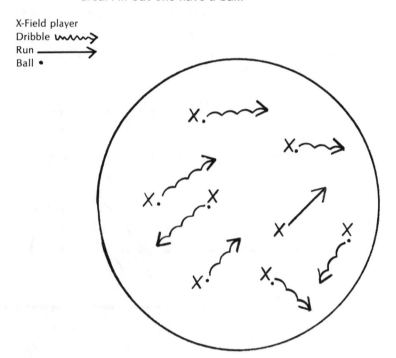

X-Field player
Dribble
Run
Ball •

Procedure: The player without a ball attempts to take a ball from any of the players who are dribbling within the area. The dribblers, in addition to not making contact with any other dribbler, try to evade the tackler by screening the ball, or changing direction or speed. Once a dribbler has lost possession of his ball he must try to take a ball from any other dribbler than the one who tackled him.

Variation: Additional players, one at a time, are without a ball until half the players are dribblers and half are tacklers.

100 QUICK SHOOTING

Shooting	½ Field	12 Players	6 Balls
		Goalkeeper	

Fitness

Formation: Offensive players line up at mid-field alongside the feeder. Defensive players form a line at the side of the field at a point eighteen yards from the goal. Two of the defensive players serve as retrievers.

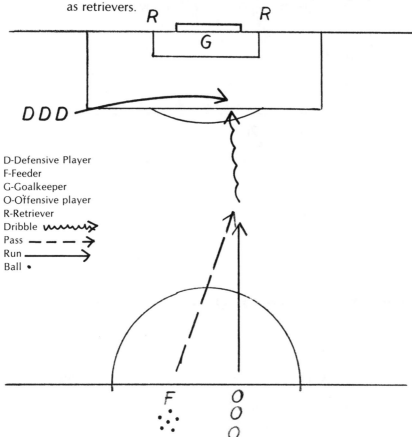

D-Defensive Player
F-Feeder
G-Goalkeeper
O-Offensive player
R-Retriever
Dribble 〰〰〰〰➤
Pass — — — →
Run ⎯⎯⎯→
Ball •

Procedure: The feeder passes the ball forward for the offensive player to dribble and shoot. At a given signal, the defender sprints to confront the offensive player. The object is for the offensive player to get a good shot on goal before being confronted by the defender.

101 RAPID FIRE

Goalkeeping	20 yd. Area in Front of Goal	10 Players	10 Balls
		Goalkeeper	Goal

Shooting

Formation: Ten field players line up 20 yards in front of a goal each with a ball at his feet. A goalkeeper is positioned in goal.

G-Goalkeeper
X-Field player
Shot ------>
Ball •

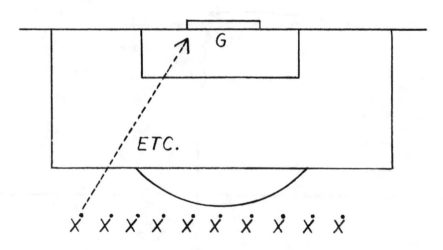

Procedure: At a signal, players shoot a stationary ball at goal. Shooting proceeds from left to right. Players wait only long enough between shots to be sure that goalkeeper has adequate time to recover from the previous shot.

102 REACTION DRIBBLE

Dribbling Any Area 2 or More Players 1 Ball
per Player

Formation: A line of players, each with a ball, is about thirty yards from the coach.

C-Coach
X-Field player
Dribble ᴜᴜᴜᴜᴜᴜᴜ⟩
Ball ➴

C) ⟵ᴜᴜᴜᴜ. X .X .X .X

Procedure: Each player, in turn, dribbles at half speed toward the coach. When the dribbler is about five feet away, the coach signals with his hand indicating to which side he wants the dribbler to pass.

Increase the dribbler's speed and decrease the distance before signalling as dribblers become more proficient.

103 REACTION DRILL

Juggling Any Area 2 Players 1 Ball

Formation: Two players, with one ball, stand about five yards apart.

X-Field player
Pass — — —⟶
Ball

X ⟵----. X

Procedure: The two players juggle between each other, but must use a different part of the body than the partner used to return the ball. The ball may be returned first time or controlled and then returned.

104 REALISTIC HEADING

Heading   5 yd. by 5 yd. Area   2 Players   3 Balls

Formation: A feeder faces a field player who is five yards away. A second field player stands directly in front of the first player also facing the feeder.

F-Feeder
X-Field player
Pass — — — →
Ball •

Procedure: The feeder serves the ball over the head of X_2. X_1 jumps and heads the ball back to the feeder.

Variation: X_2 jumps up and down as the ball is being served. Jumping provides a more realistic situation for X_1.

105 RECEIVE AND SHOOT

Shooting   30 yd. by 20 yd. Area   2 Players   10 Balls

2 Goalkeepers   2 Goals

Defensive Techniques

Formation: Two field players stand in the middle of the playing area facing each other and a goal. A feeder serves a ball between them. Goalkeepers are in each goal.

F-Feeder
G-Goalkeeper
X-Field player
Pass — — — →
Ball •

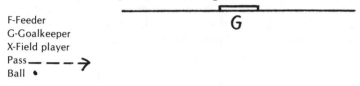

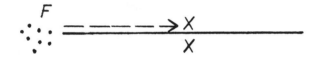

Procedure: The feeder serves the ball between the two players. The player gaining control immediately shoots at the goal he is facing. The other player defends against the shot. As soon as one ball is used i.e., goes out of play, another ball is served.

Variation: Assign two players to each team and permit a pass before the shot.

106 REWARD THE SHOOTER

Shooting   Penalty Area   12 Players   10 Balls

                                      Goalkeeper   Scrimmage
                                                        Vests
Passing

CONTRIBUTOR: Ronald Cervasio, Boston University, Boston,
Massachusetts 02215

Formation: Pairs of players form a semi-circle in front of a goal. Another
pair of players position themselves about eight yards from the
goal. A goalkeeper is in the goal. Two feeders, each with five
balls, stand off the field by a goalpost.

B-Player wearing
  blue vest
G-Goalkeeper
W-Player wearing
  white vest
Pass — — — →
Ball •

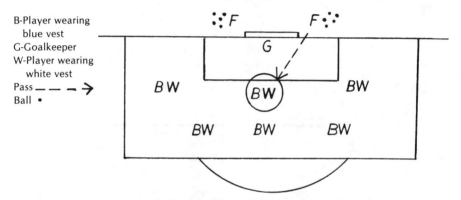

Procedure: One of the feeders passes a ball to the players who are eight
yards in front of the goal. The player gaining possession attempts to shoot on goal, while the other player assumes a defensive role and attempts to dispossess the offensive player of the
ball. If successful the player gaining possession attempts to
shoot on goal. After shooting the player attempts to free himself
to receive another ball from either one of the feeders. The
player in the center in possession of the ball may pass to other
players on the semi-circle around him who are wearing the same
color vest. The supporting player who received the pass may
pass back (give and go) to the center player. Players on the semi-
circle cannot steal balls from each other or from players in the
middle. After ten balls are played, the pair in the center moves
to the semi-circle while another pair goes to the center.

107 RIGHT ANGLES

Passing   10 yd. by 10 yd. Area   4 Players   1 Ball

Movement Without the Ball

Formation: Three players start at any three corners of area and try to keep the ball away from one defender.

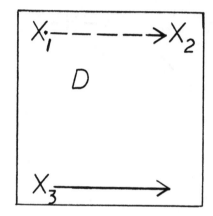

Procedure: Each time an X has the ball, the other two X's should be at right angles to him. For example, X_1 has the ball and can pass to either X_2 or X_3 who are both at right angles to him. As X_1 passes the ball to X_2, X_3 runs to a new position and X_2 now has two players at right angles to him.

Variation: 1. Depending on skill level, D should offer passive or active defense.
2. Start with a specific control and pass restriction and move to one touch play.

108 SARDINES

Passing   Center Circle   12-24 Players   4 Balls

Scrimmage
Vests

CONTRIBUTOR: George R. Logan, San Diego State University,
San Diego, California 92182

Formation: Four squads of three to six players each are located within the center circle or similar size area. Each squad wears different colored bibs and has one ball, which should be a different color than the others.

B-Player with blue vest
G-Player with green vest
R-Player with red vest
Y-Player with yellow vest
Ball •

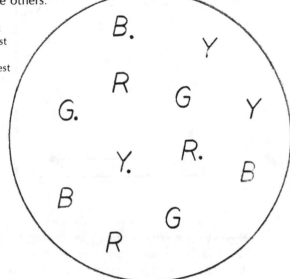

Procedure: The players interpass among their own squad. After a period of unlimited passing, different restrictions can be introduced such as one touch, two touch, and left or right foot only.

Variation: 1. The players in each squad try to knock the other balls out of the area using their own ball as a "cannon" (no kicking the balls out).

2. One player in each squad stops the ball dead and calls a teammate's name. That player must instantly sprint to the ball and continue passing.

3. Passes must be made from one player to another in a specified sequence.

109 SEE MAN AND BALL

Defensive Techniques   Any Area   5 Players   1 Ball

Formation: O_1, with a ball, is about fifteen yards away from O_2. D_1 and D_2 are marking O_1 and O_2 respectively while D_3 provides cover.

D-Defensive player
O-Offensive player
Pass — — — →
Run ———→
Ball •

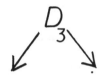

Procedure: O_1 and O_2 interpass slowly. D_1 and D_2 move to alternately mark and support as ball moves toward and away from man. D_3 moves to proper cover position.

110 SHOOTING THROUGH GATES

Shooting	Penalty Area	10 Players	10 Balls
		Goalkeeper	4 Cones
Dribbling			
Passing			1 Goal

CONTRIBUTOR: Fred Schmalz, University of Evansville, Evansville, Indiana 47702

Formation: A line of players is located at each corner of one end line. A gate (five yards wide marked by two cones) is located a few yards outside each of the penalty area corners furthest from the goal.

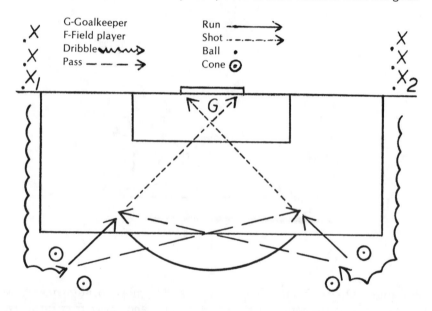

Procedure: X_1 and X_2 simultaneously dribble the ball at top speed from the corners to the nearest gate. Running wide of the gates they drive a low cross through the gates toward the opposite corner of the penalty area. Following their passes, each player sprints to the ball crossed by the other player and takes a first time shot on goal.

The drill may be performed with or without goalkeepers. Players rotate to the opposite corner after each turn.

111 SHOOT IN STRIDE

Shooting	¼ Field	12 Players	12 Balls
Goalkeeping		Goalkeeper	1 Goal

Formation: The players, each with a ball, form two equal lines about thirty yards from goal.

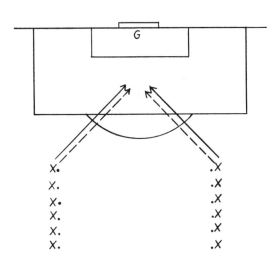

Procedure: Each player, in turn and alternating lines, pushes the ball forward on the ground and sprints after it. The player is to shoot as soon as he reaches the ball without breaking stride, using whichever foot is appropriate. Avoid dribbling or setting up for "best" foot. Shots should be taken from about the eighteen yard line, but no closer than the twelve yard line. Each player retrieves his own shot and, staying out of the shooting area, returns to the end of the opposite line.

Variation: 1. Each player lobs ball forward, chases and shoots on volley or half-volley. The ball should be thrown just high enough to reach and shoot without slowing down.

2. The second player in line passes the ball through the legs of the first player, who sprints after it and shoots.

3. Repeat #2, with the first player facing the second player, turning and running after pass through his legs.

131

112 SHOOT WITH OPPOSITION

Shooting   Penalty Area   8-24 Players   10 Balls

1-3 Goalkeepers

Defensive Techniques

Formation: Defensive players form two lines, one behind each goalpost. Offensive players form two lines at the outer corners of the penalty area. A goalkeeper is in the goal. Five balls are off the field of play by each post.

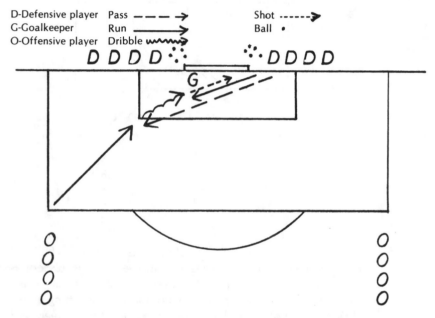

D-Defensive player   Pass — — — →   Shot ------→
G-Goalkeeper   Run ———→   Ball •
O-Offensive player   Dribble 〰〰〰→

Procedure: The first man in one of the defensive lines passes the ball to the first offensive player in the diagonally opposite line. The defensive player then runs to defend against the offensive player who attempts to score. After the play, the defensive player goes to the end of the other defensive line and the offensive player goes to the end of the other offensive line.

Variation: 1. A feeder serves high balls to offensive players to be headed on goal.
2. Players rotate in a clockwise manner to the end of the line. In this way all players play offense and defense.

113 SHORT AND LONG

Fitness   Any Area   2 Players   1 Ball

Passing

Formation: X_1, with a ball, stands about ten feet away from and facing X_2.

X-Field player
Pass — — — →
Run ——————→
Ball •

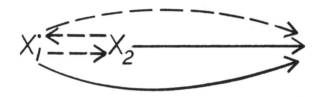

Procedure: X_1 makes a ground pass to X_2 and receives a first time ground pass back. X_1 then makes a chip pass over the head of X_2 and about 30 yards beyond him. X_2 turns and runs to control the long pass. X_1 follows X_2 and should be about ten feet away when X_2 controls the ball. The drill is then repeated.

114 SHUTTLE SPRINTS

Fitness   15 Yd. Area   8 or More Players   None

Formation: Eight players stand in two lines fifteen yards apart.

X-Field Player
Run ———————→

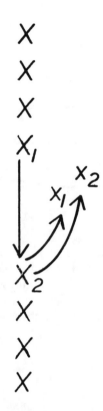

Procedure: X_1 starts by sprinting across to X_2 and tags him. As in a relay, X_2 than starts to sprint to the other side. However, immediately after tagging X_2, X_1 sprints back after him, returning to the end of his original line and waits his turn to be tagged and chased by a player from the other line.

The sprints can continue for a specified time or until each player has made a specified number of runs.

115 SIT UP HEADING

Fitness   Any Area   2 or More Players   1 Ball
                                                                 per pair
Heading

Formation: X₁ is in a sit-up position with hands at side. His partner, X₂, with a soccer ball, stands about 10 feet from the feet of X₁.

X-Field player
Pass __ __ __ →
Ball •

Procedure: X₁ begins performing sit-ups. X₂ throws the ball underhand to X₁, timing the throw so X₁ can head the ball each time he reaches the sitting position. This continues for thirty seconds, after which the players change positions.

This drill can be done one or more times in-between some form of sprinting or running.

116 SPRINT AND HEAD

Fitness   15 yd. by 15 yd. Area   3 Players   6 Balls

                                                     1 Cone

Heading   1 Goal

Formation: One player, X_1, is on a line ten yards from a goal (or wall). A cone is five yards further from the goal. Two other players, X_2 and X_3, are in front of each side of the goal.

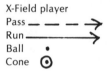

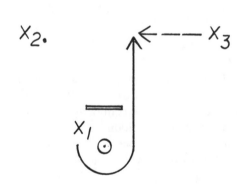

Procedure: On signal, X_1 sprints around cone and towards goal where he heads balls thrown alternately by X_2 and X_3. The balls should be thrown so that X_1 does not have to slow down and has to jump head each ball. One ball is to be headed over the goal and the other into the goal. X_1 continues sprinting and heading for forty-five seconds after which the players change positions.

Record the number of balls headed within the time period.

117 SPRINT AND SHOOT

Fitness   15 yd. by 15 yd. Area   3 Players   3 Balls

1 Cone

Shooting   1 Small Goal

Formation: Two players, X_1 and X_2, are on a line ten yards from a small goal or wall. A cone is five yards further from the goal. A third player, X_3, stands near the goal.

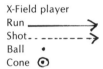

X-Field player
Run ⟶
Shot ⟶
Ball •
Cone ⊙

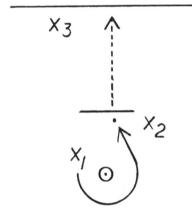

Procedure: On signal, X_1 sprints around cone and back to line where he shoots ball placed on line by X_2. X_1 continues sprinting and shooting for forty-five seconds. X_3 retrieves balls and passes them to X_2. X_1 should not have to wait for a ball to shoot, and if one is not ready on the line, he should again sprint around the cone.
Rotate positions after forty-five seconds.

Variation: 1. To emphasize conditioning, record the number of shots taken within the time period.
2. To emphasize shooting, record the number of goals made within the time period.

137

118 SPRINT TO BALL

Fitness   50 yd. by 10 yd. Area   4-16 Field Players   12 Balls

---

Formation: Two lines of field players are formed with a feeder and a supply of balls between them.

F-Feeder
X-Field player
Pass— — — →
Run ——————→
Ball •

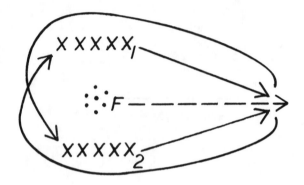

Procedure: The feeder sends a pass downfield. At a signal, X₁ and X₂ sprint to the ball. The player gaining possession dribbles the ball back to the feeder. Players, after their turn, return to the end of the opposite line.

Variation: The player not getting to the ball first, takes the ball and dribbles one lap around the field.

119 SPRINT TO DEFENSE

Offensive and Defensive Techniques	½ Field	12 or More Players	3 Balls
		Goalkeeper	2 Cones
Fitness			Goal
Goalkeeping			

Formation: Four or more defensive players line up behind one goal post. Eight or more offensive players form two lines at mid-field about ten yards to each side of the center circle. A goalkeeper is in goal. Cones are placed at points three yards from the outer marking of the penalty area, about three yards from the end line.

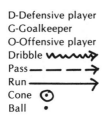

D-Defensive player
G-Goalkeeper
O-Offensive player
Dribble
Pass
Run
Cone
Ball

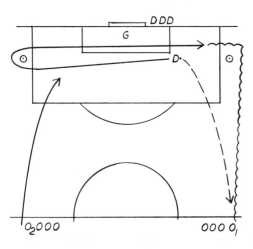

Procedure: A defensive player kicks a goalkick to O₁ who is waiting at mid-field. O₁ receives the ball and dribbles down around the cone on the same side of the field. After he dribbles around the cone, he attempts to cross the ball to O₂ who has made a run to the far post. The defensive player, after taking the goalkick, sprints across the penalty area, around the cone and back to the other cone to confront O₁ who is attempting to cross the ball. If O₂ receives the ball from the cross he attempts to score. The goalkeeper attempts to intercept the cross, or if this fails, stop the shot.

Variation: The location of the cones may be changed

120 STAY WIDE

Offensive and *Defensive Techniques*	40 yd. by 20 yd. *Area*	8 Players	1 Ball
			2 Small *Goals*

Formation: The basic set-up is a three vs three game in a 40 yd. X 20 yd. area with small goals. Two offensive players are added near the touch lines.

O-Offensive player
D-Defensive player

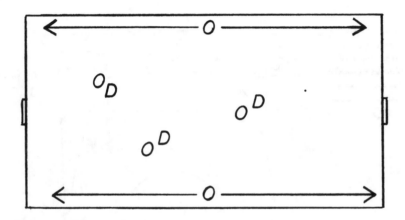

Procedure: The wings play in the same direction as the team in possession of the ball (i.e., the wings are always on attack). When used, the wings may only cross the ball.

121 STEAL THE BACON

Offensive and   Penalty Area   10 Players   5 Balls
Defensive Techniques

                         2 Goalkeepers   2Goals

                                          10 Scrimmage
                                           Vests

CONTRIBUTOR: William Muse, Princeton University, Princeton, New Jersey 08540

Formation: The penalty area of similar size area can be used as a field with two portable goals. There are two teams of equal numbers. Each team stands off the field by its goal. The players on each team are assigned corresponding numbers. A goalkeeper is in each goal. A feeder, with a supply of balls, stands at the side of mid-field.

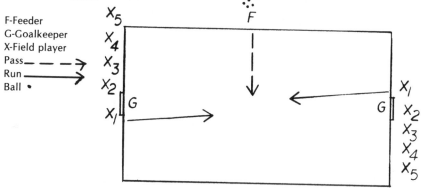

F-Feeder
G-Goalkeeper
X-Field player
Pass‑ ‑ ‑ ‑→
Run ──→
Ball •

Procedure: The feeder plays a ball into the middle of the field and calls a number. (E.G."3"). A player with the assigned number from each team runs to the center. The player who gains possession of the ball attacks the opposing goal and the other player defends. A one vs one situation continues until a goal is scored or the ball goes out of bounds. When this happens, the feeder plays another ball into the middle and calls a new number.

Variation: 1. More than one number can be called to create two vs two, three vs three, etc., situations.
2. The players try to get the ball back to the goal on the line from which they came.

141

122 SUPPORT

Support	Wide Open Area	4-24 Players	1 Ball for Every Group

Movement With/
Without the Ball

Formation: Four players line up with three players in a line about five yards apart. One player, X₄, is five yards behind the middle player, X₁, who has a ball.

X-Field player
Dribble ∿∿∿⟿
Pass — — — ⟿
Run———⟶
Ball •

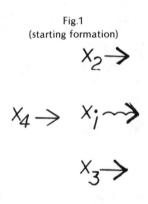

Fig.1
(starting formation)

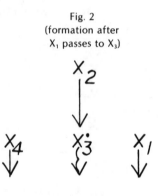

Fig. 2
(formation after
X₁ passes to X₃)

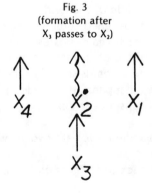

Fig. 3
(formation after
X₃ passes to X₂)

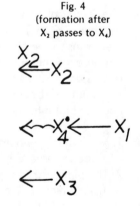

Fig. 4
(formation after
X₂ passes to X₄)

Procedure: The player with the ball dribbles, while the players to his side and behind run along in the same direction keeping the original formation. X_1 passes to anyone of his supporting players. The player receiving the ball continues dribbling following the path of the passed ball. The other players assume the supporting position which involves the least movement.

Variation: A defensive player may be introduced. His objective is to intercept a pass. If the support is accomplished this task should be very difficult.

123 TACKLE IN CONFINED AREA

Tackling   5 yd. by 5 yd. Area   4-12 Players   3 Balls

Offensive Techniques

Formation: Four cones define a course five yards wide by ten yards long. Dribblers line up at the entrance to the course. Tacklers line up at the exit.

D-Defensive player
O-Offensive player
Dribble 〰〰〰➤
Run ————➤
Cone •

ⵙ   ⵙ

OOOOO 〰〰〰➤<————DDDDD

ⵙ   ⵙ

Procedure: Each offensive player attempts to dribble, staying within the course, through the distant two cones. The defensive player tries to prevent the offensive player from dribbling through the course by accomplishing a legal tackle. At the conclusion of each turn the players go to the the end of the other line.

124 THREE BALL DRILL

Passing   Center Circle   10 Players   3 Balls

Formation: Ten players form a circle around the center circle (or similar size area). Three players have soccer balls.

X-Field player
Pass — — — →
Ball •

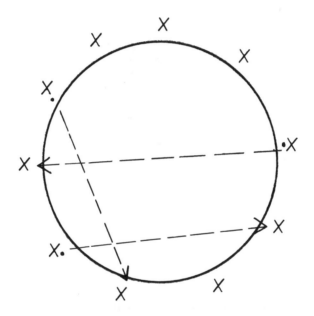

Procedure: The three balls are passed at the same time. Continued passes should be made first time or a control may be allowed. Players should make ground passes to other player's feet.

125 THREE MAN SKILL WORK

Offensive and	Any Area	3 Players	2 Balls
Defensive Techniques			per Group

Formation: Two field players each with a ball face a third player.

X-Field player
Pass — — — →

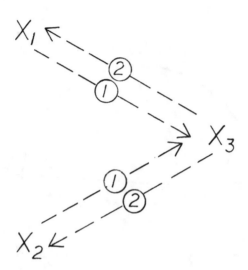

Procedure: Players X_1 and X_2 in turn serve balls to X_3. X_3 returns balls for 1 minute by head, instep volley, and instep half volley passes. The balls are then served to the chest of X_3 who controls the balls to his feet and makes volley and half volley return passes. After X_3 has practiced all the skills, he switches places with X_3. Later X_2 switches with X_1.

126 THROW-HEAD-CATCH

Heading	¼ Field	12 Players	1 Ball
Fitness			2 Small Goals
Marking			

Formation: Each team consists of six players who are in their own half until the game starts. There are no goalkeepers.

D-Defensive player
O-Offensive player
Pass — — — →
Ball •

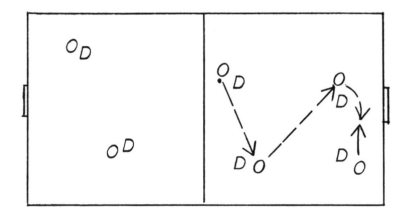

Procedure: Play is started by a throw from mid-field. Play may proceed in any direction but must follow a throw-head-catch sequence. Any type of throw is legal. No more than three steps are permitted before throwing the ball. One player may not touch the ball twice in succession. Goals are scored only by heading.
Defenders may closely mark but not take the ball away from the thrower. Possession is lost if the proper sequence is interrupted or the defense intercepts. The ball may not touch the ground.

127 THROWING ON THE MOVE

Fitness   ½ Field   3 Players   2 Balls

Heading

Formation: Two players, X_2 and X_3, each with a ball, are on the end line facing X_1, who is five feet away with his back to mid-field.

X-Field player
Pass — — — →
Run ————→
Ball •

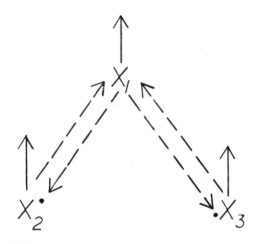

Procedure: X_2 and X_3 alternate throws to X_1 who heads the passes back to each player. X_2 and X_3 are running forward and X_1 backward throughout the drill. When the players reach mid-field, they change positions and return to the start performing the same drill. The drill is done twice by each player.

148

128 THROW-RECEIVE-DRIBBLE

Throwing   30 yd. by 10 yd. Area   16 Players   1-3 Balls

Dribbling
Receiving

Formation: Two lines of field players, 20 yards apart, face each other. The first player in one of the lines has a ball.

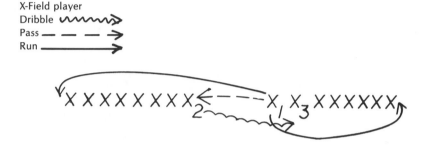

X-Field player
Dribble
Pass
Run

Procedure: The first player on line, X_1, throws to the head, chest or feet of the first player on the opposite line, X_2. X_2 dribbles across to X_3. X_1 and X_2 go to the end of the opposite line, and the drill is repeated with the two new front players.

129 TURN AND HEAD

Heading   10 yd. by 10 yd. Area   3 Players   2 Balls

Fitness

Formation: Two players, (X_2 and X_3) each with a ball, stand ten yards apart. A third player, X_1, is in the center facing X_2.

X-Field Player
Pass
Ball

Procedure: X_2 throws to X_1 who jumps to head the ball back to X_2, then turns quickly to jump head a ball already thrown by X_3. The throws should be accurate and timed so that X_1 is forced to jump head and turn quickly. The ball should already be in flight as X_1 turns. Start slowly and build up speed. Rotate positions after forty-five seconds.

130 TURN AND SHOOT

Shooting   Penalty Area   10 Players   10 Balls

Defensive Techniques   Goalkeeper   Goal
Fitness, Goalkeeping

Formation: A feeder stands about twenty yards from the goal. An offensive player stands near the penalty spot. A defensive player marks the offensive player. A goalkeeper is in goal. Waiting defensive players serve as retrievers behind the goal. Waiting offensive players help the feeder by supplying balls.

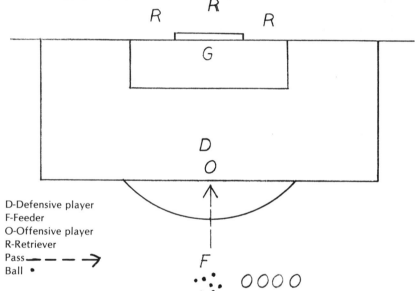

D-Defensive player
F-Feeder
O-Offensive player
R-Retriever
Pass ▬ ▬ ▬ ⟶
Ball •

Procedure: The feeder serves a ball to the offensive player who shoots on goal as soon as possible. After the shot is taken the feeder serves another ball. The offensive player is under constant pressure provided by the defensive player. Each offensive player receives balls continuously for one minute.

Variation: 1. Offensive player receives balls for one minute *or* until a goal is scored.
2. Add competitive element by keeping track of the number of goals scored in the designated time.
3. Increase time to one and one half or two minutes.
4. Two offensive players are used. The player receiving the ball from the feeder passes, first time, to his teammate who plays on goal.

131 TURN AND VOLLEY

Shooting	25 yds. in Front of a Goal	8 Players	6 Balls
		Goalkeeper	Goal

Formation: Offensive players form a line twenty-five yards from the goal. The first player in line faces a feeder. A goalkeeper is in goal.

F-Feeder
G-Goalkeeper
O-Offensive player
Pass ___ ___ ___ →
Run _____→
Shot............→

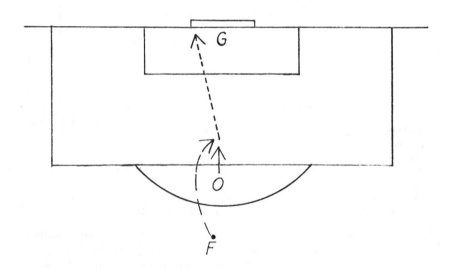

Procedure: The feeder lofts the ball over the head of the offensive player, who turns and moves to the ball shooting as the ball rebounds from the ground (half-volley).

Variation: Serve for left, then right foot shot.

152

132 TWO TOUCH-ERROR EXPELS

Passing   Full Field   22 Players   3 Balls

2 Goalkeepers

Formation: Players in scrimmage vests, line up in game formation, i.e.; eleven vs eleven. Each team has at least one substitute.

Procedure: A game of soccer is played with one restriction - the ball may only be touched two times in succession by any one player (goalkeepers are exempt from this restriction). If a player touches the ball three times in succession, he is expelled and is immediately replaced by the substitute.

Variation: 1. Field players may not touch ball twice in succession, i.e. one touch soccer.
2. Forwards may be allowed more touches if the play ends with a shot on goal.
3. Less than eleven man sides may be used i.e. six vs six, seven vs seven, eight vs eight.

133 TWO vs ONE

Passing	15 yd. by 15 yd. Area	8 Players	1 Ball

Formation: Eight players stand in two lines fifteen yards apart.

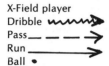

X-Field player
Dribble
Pass
Run
Ball •

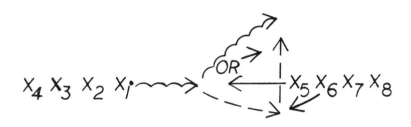

Procedure: X_1 dribbles toward X_5 who is moving forward to pressure him. X_6 moves to make a passing angle for X_1. X_1 works a give and go with X_6, or keeps and dribbles past X_5. He then passes to X_7 and goes to the end of that line. X_5 and X_6 go to the end of the other line. The drill is repeated as X_7 dribbles toward X_2 with X_3 creating the passing angle.

134 TWO vs TWO COMMUNICATION

Communication	10 yd. by 20 yd. Area	6 Players	1 Ball

Offensive and 8 Cones
Defensive Techniques
Passing

CONTRIBUTOR: Loren Kline, University of Delaware, Newark, Delaware
19711

Formation: Two offensive and two defensive players are within a small field.
One feeder stands within each goal of two cones.

D-Defensive player
F-Feeder
O-Offensive player
Dribble
Pass
Run
Cone

Procedure: One of the feeders passes to an open offensive player. As the
feeder passes, he calls "man on" if the intended receiver is tight-
ly marked. In this situation the offensive player can pass back to
the feeder. If the offensive player has room the feeder calls
"hold", "turn", or "through" depending on the situation. On any
of these three calls, the feeder moves into the field to create a
three on two situation as his team attacks the small goal at the
opposite end of the field. If the defense wins the ball they
counter attack. The feeder on the team that is defending may
function as a goalkeeper but is limited to the use of his feet in
defending his goal. During counter attacks, the feeder becomes
a supporting field player. If a goal is scored or the ball crosses
the end line, the defending feeder starts the play from his end.
Offensive and defensive roles now change.

Variation: 1. Play one vs one, plus feeder in a smaller area.
2. Build up to three vs three or four vs four in a larger area.

135 TWO vs TWO PRESSURE

Shooting	Penalty Area	4 Players	8 Balls
		2 Goalkeepers	2 Goals
Receiving			

CONTRIBUTOR: Thomas Griffith, Dartmouth College, Hanover, New Hampshire 03755

Formation: Two players, X_1 and X_2, compete against two others, X_3 and X_4, in the penalty area with two full size goals and two goalkeepers. A portable goal or two sticks can be used for the second goal. A feeder, with a supply of balls, is located outside the penalty area. Players not competing serve as retrievers for the feeder.

F-Feeder   X-Field player
G-Goalkeeper   Ball •
R-Retriever

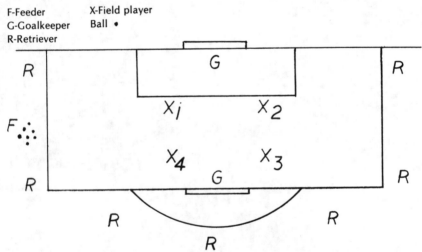

Procedure: Each pair tries to score in the appropriate goal. This is a pressure drill and balls are fed constantly giving the players no rest for three to five minutes. The balls should be fed to force various types of shots. Goal saves are rolled to a teammate and play continues. A new ball is fed in as soon as a goal is scored or a ball goes out of bounds.

Variation: 1. Feed ground balls.
2. Feed air balls.
3. Feed hard driven balls.
4. Feed a variety of balls

136 WALL PASS GAME

Passing   Center Circle   4 Players   1 Ball

4 Cones

Formation: Use the center circle, or other similar size area for a small field. Make two goals about a yard wide opposite each other on the edge of the circle. Play two vs. two games within the area.

D-Defensive player
O-Offensive player
Pass — — — ⇾
Run ——————⇾
Shot – – – – – – – ⇾
Ball •
Cone ⊙

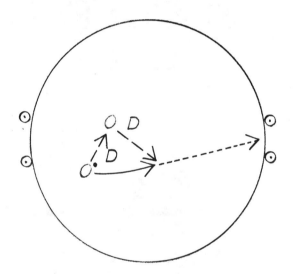

Procedure: The only way to score is directly from a wall pass maneuver with the player who receives the return pass shooting.

The Coaches Collection
of
SOCCER
DRILLS